13 FROM THE SWAMP
Passaic River Lore
©2019 Wheeler Antabanez
ISBN-13: 978-1092371681
Text Copyright ©2019 Wheeler Antabanez
Photography Copyright ©2019 Wheeler Antabanez
Design and Layout Copyright ©2019 Wheeler Antabanez
All photography by Wheeler Antabanez unless otherwise noted
Published independently by Wheeler Antabanez
2019 First Edition

Dedicated to the memory of

X. Ray Burns

Sunday will never be the same

IBJ Forever!

"Wheeeeeee"

CONTENTS

Introduction

From afar, New Jerseyans stare at the swamp. We shirk from slogging through the muck, the clinging mud, the spatters of malevolence sunk not-so-deep.

Wheeler Antabanez doesn't recoil from the wretchedness. Within the abandoned riverfront factories and architectural detritus, Wheeler spots the subtle signs of continuity from a much earlier age: the solitary bird, a flowering bush, a creature not yet killed.

With black-enameled fingernails, Wheeler steers his canoe into debris-entangled coves, chancing upon once-relevant ruins. Adventuring into places whose significance has devolved into nothingness.

He grabs images of the abandoned, he captures videos of desolation, he conjures words and stanzas depicting the swirling water and the depths of the darkness.

Flexing those black-enameled fingers and his acute, nocturnal sensitivity, Wheeler's mixed a strange brew of "13 From The Swamp".

Ingredients are plucked from a silence that seethes, from overgrown shorelines, half-collapsed moorings and remnants of voodoo rituals.

Our doors locked, we can safely sip on Wheeler's luminous observations of the lurid and the stillborn.

Wheeler, however, is motoring into another unnamed cove, minimizing his wake.

-Mark S. Porter-
Editor In Chief Emeritus
The Montclair Times

SWAMP WINTER

Passaic River banks

In winter

Where fluctuating water levels

Form impromptu ice sculptures

So complex

Fragile

And temporary

That even the slight wake

From the *Nightshade*

Makes the ice shiver

And sometimes shatter

As my gloved hands clutch the paddle

Passing it back and forth

From gunwale to gunwale

Dipping silently into polluted water

Propelling the canoe steadily upstream

In a fine flurry of snow

Smell of January on the cold breeze

Accented by wood smoke

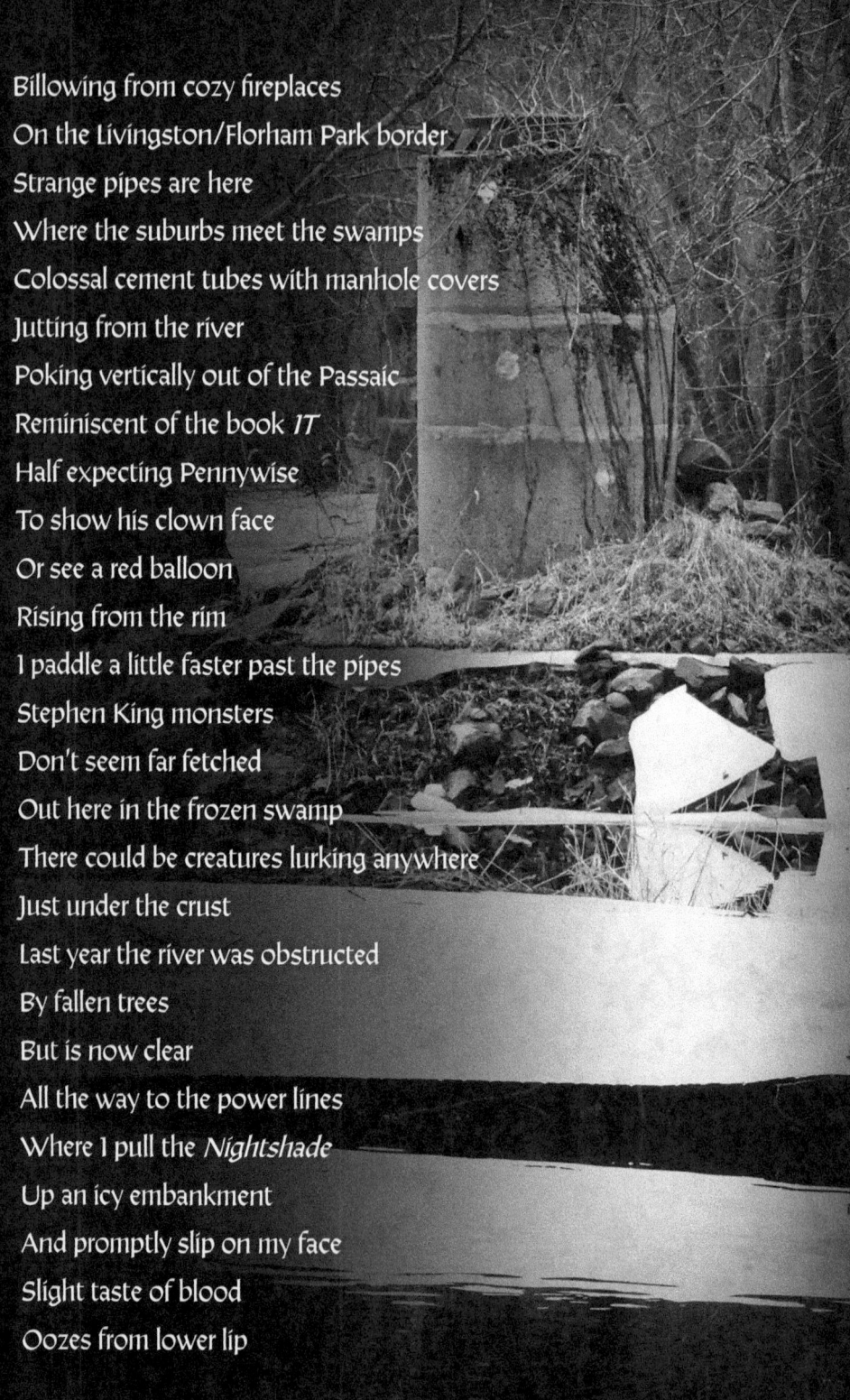

Billowing from cozy fireplaces

On the Livingston/Florham Park border

Strange pipes are here

Where the suburbs meet the swamps

Colossal cement tubes with manhole covers

Jutting from the river

Poking vertically out of the Passaic

Reminiscent of the book *IT*

Half expecting Pennywise

To show his clown face

Or see a red balloon

Rising from the rim

I paddle a little faster past the pipes

Stephen King monsters

Don't seem far fetched

Out here in the frozen swamp

There could be creatures lurking anywhere

Just under the crust

Last year the river was obstructed

By fallen trees

But is now clear

All the way to the power lines

Where I pull the *Nightshade*

Up an icy embankment

And promptly slip on my face

Slight taste of blood

Oozes from lower lip

But no, I'm OK
I stow the canoe and start walking
Trudging from hummock
To frozen hummock
Toward looming high-tension wires
An off-limits zone
Where towers zap electricity
And steadily hummmmm
As they march through the swamp
I follow a gravel utility road
Leading to an abandoned farmhouse
Overgrown with vines
Windows boarded up
Doors open to the elements
Spooky
Sagging
Secluded
And now I'm inside
Crunching around on broken glass
Making sure no one is home
Before creaking up rickety stairs
To check out the second floor
Where bedrooms are ransacked
And mildewed wallpaper peels
Smelling strongly of urine
Another staircase leads to the farmhouse attic
I put my boot on the first step

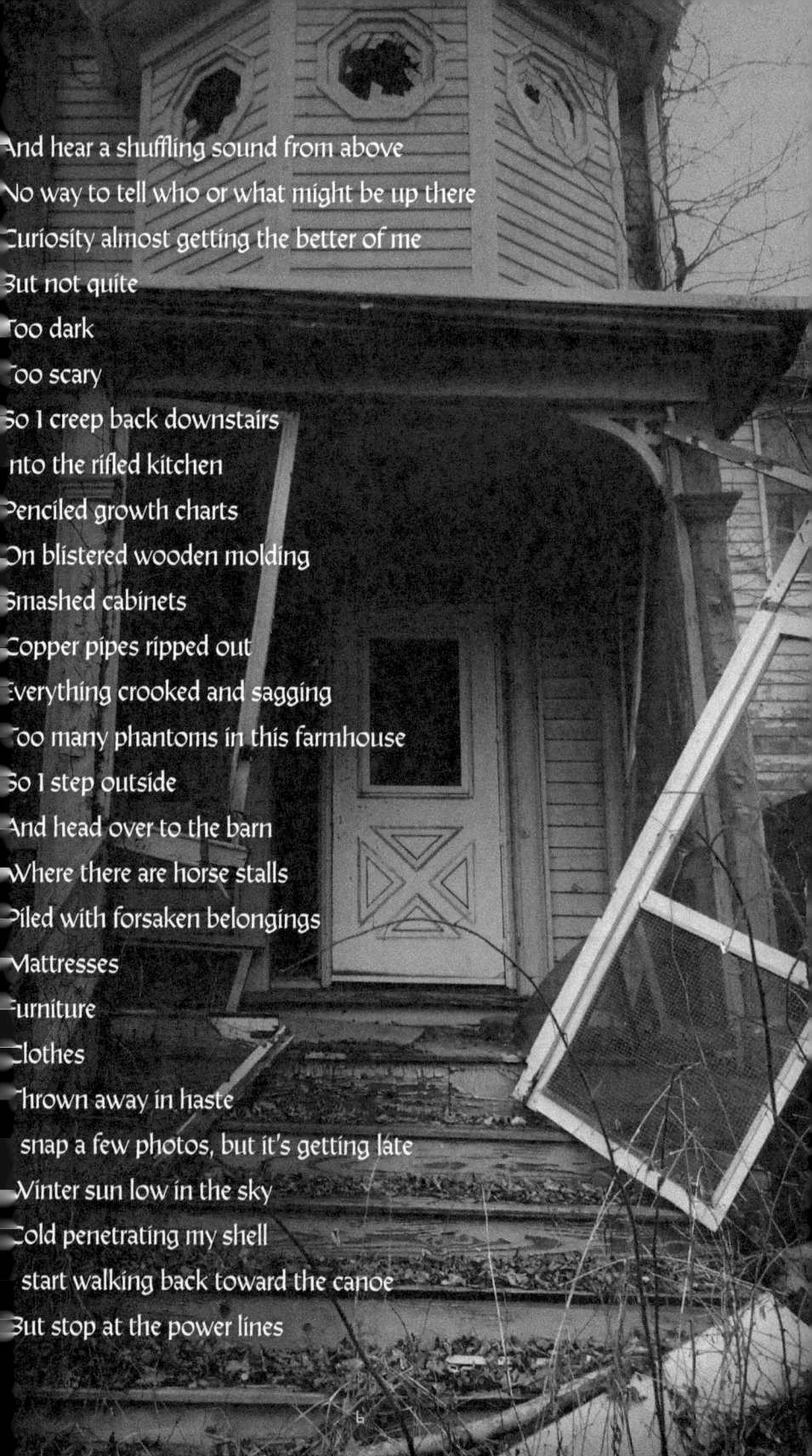

And hear a shuffling sound from above
No way to tell who or what might be up there
Curiosity almost getting the better of me
But not quite
Too dark
Too scary
So I creep back downstairs
Into the rifled kitchen
Penciled growth charts
On blistered wooden molding
Smashed cabinets
Copper pipes ripped out
Everything crooked and sagging
Too many phantoms in this farmhouse
So I step outside
And head over to the barn
Where there are horse stalls
Piled with forsaken belongings
Mattresses
Furniture
Clothes
Thrown away in haste
I snap a few photos, but it's getting late
Winter sun low in the sky
Cold penetrating my shell
I start walking back toward the canoe
But stop at the power lines

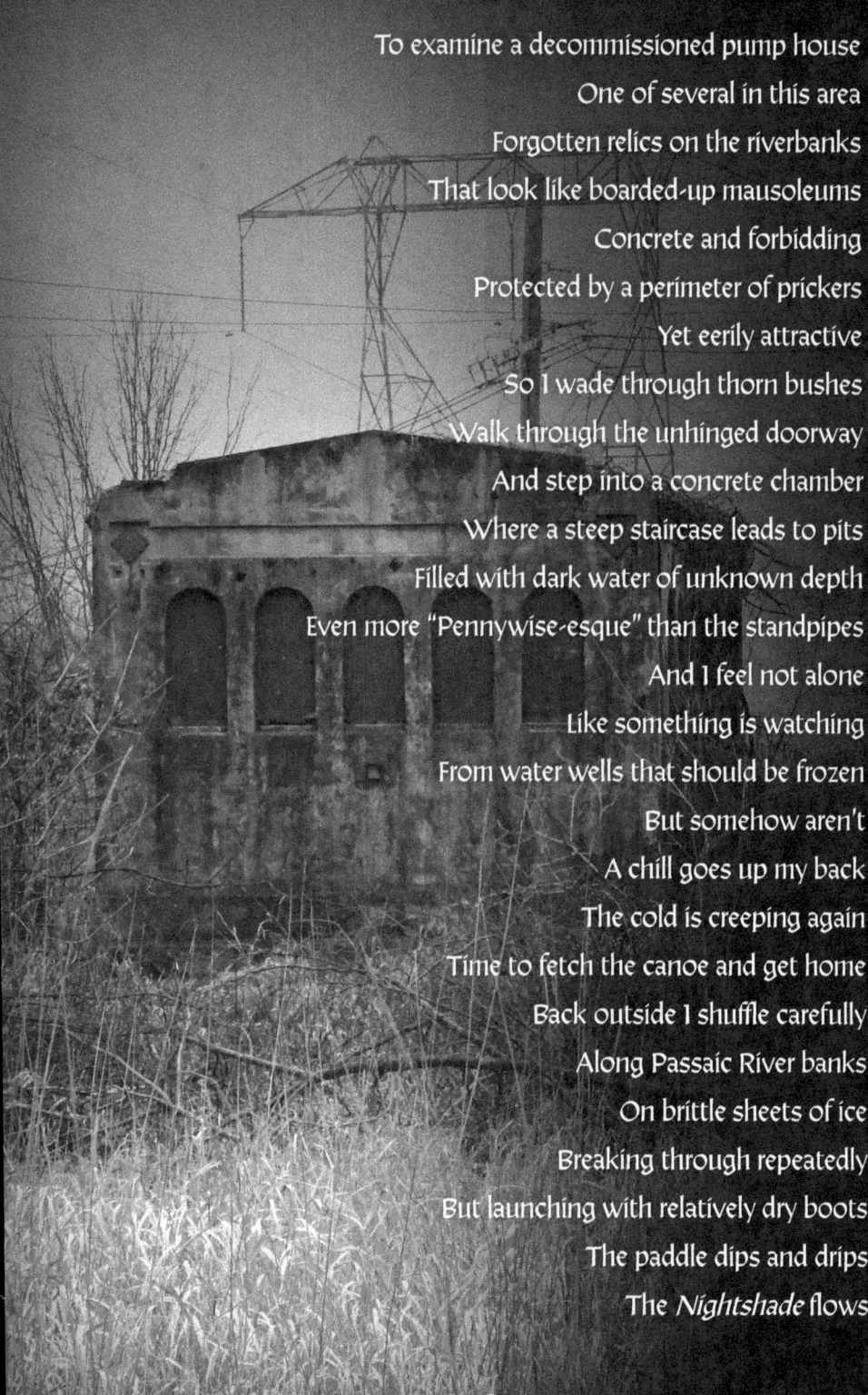

To examine a decommissioned pump house
One of several in this area
Forgotten relics on the riverbanks
That look like boarded-up mausoleums
Concrete and forbidding
Protected by a perimeter of prickers
Yet eerily attractive
So I wade through thorn bushes
Walk through the unhinged doorway
And step into a concrete chamber
Where a steep staircase leads to pits
Filled with dark water of unknown depth
Even more "Pennywise-esque" than the standpipes
And I feel not alone
Like something is watching
From water wells that should be frozen
But somehow aren't
A chill goes up my back
The cold is creeping again
Time to fetch the canoe and get home
Back outside I shuffle carefully
Along Passaic River banks
On brittle sheets of ice
Breaking through repeatedly
But launching with relatively dry boots
The paddle dips and drips
The *Nightshade* flows

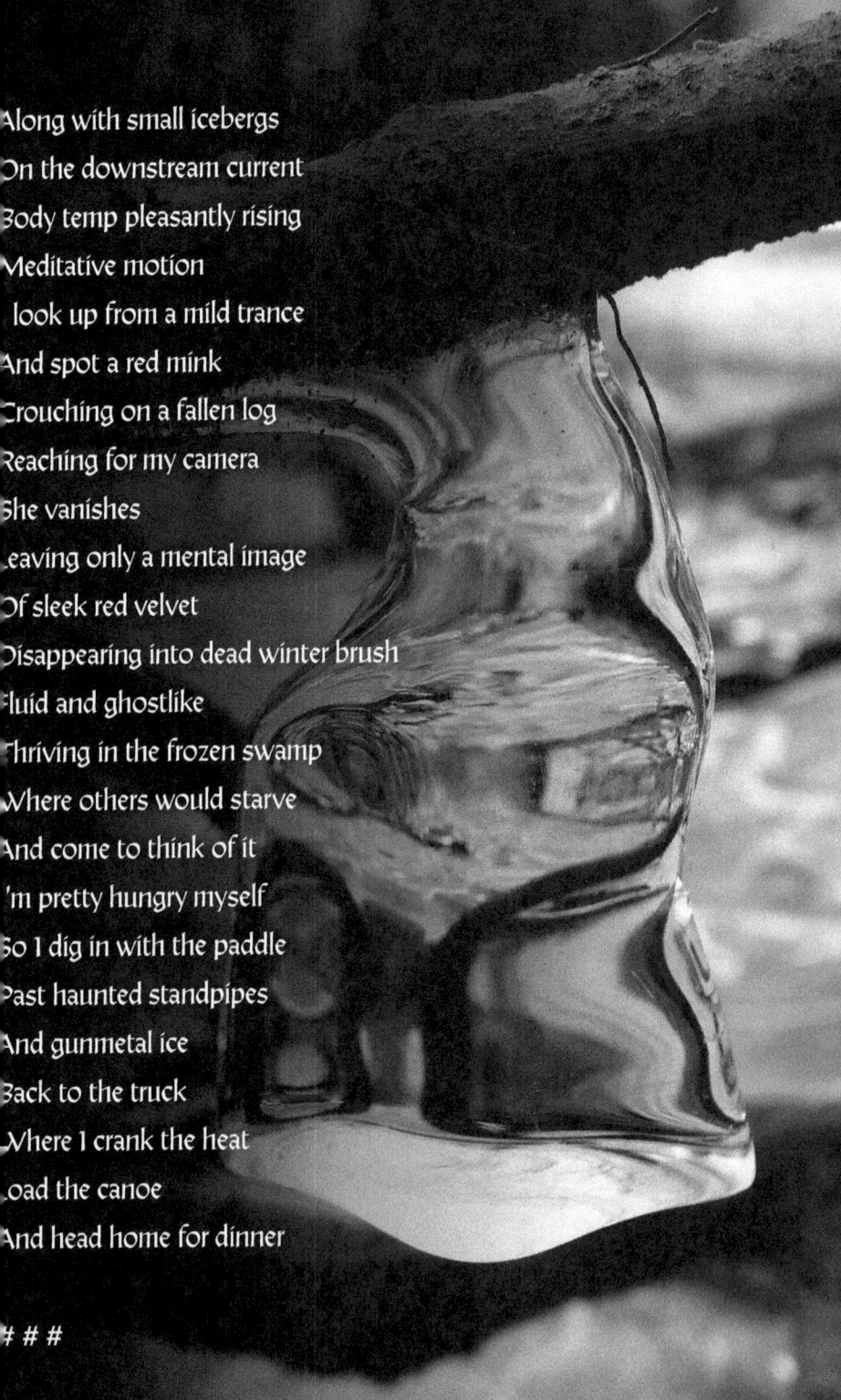

Along with small icebergs
On the downstream current
Body temp pleasantly rising
Meditative motion
  look up from a mild trance
And spot a red mink
Crouching on a fallen log
Reaching for my camera
She vanishes
Leaving only a mental image
Of sleek red velvet
Disappearing into dead winter brush
Fluid and ghostlike
Thriving in the frozen swamp
Where others would starve
And come to think of it
I'm pretty hungry myself
So I dig in with the paddle
Past haunted standpipes
And gunmetal ice
Back to the truck
Where I crank the heat
Load the canoe
And head home for dinner

# # #

RIVER OF DEATH

Cruising with my wife in the speedboat

On the Passaic River

One fine summer morning in 2012

Approaching Diamond Shamrock

In Newark, New Jersey

Where the EPA is dredging

To remove dioxin-contaminated mud

Behind 80 Lister Avenue

Once the site of a notorious chemical factory

That was dismantled in the year 2000

By men in space suits

Who packed

932 shipping containers

With toxic rubble

And entombed them in place

Beneath a monumental Superfund cap

The Diamond plant originally manufactured DDT

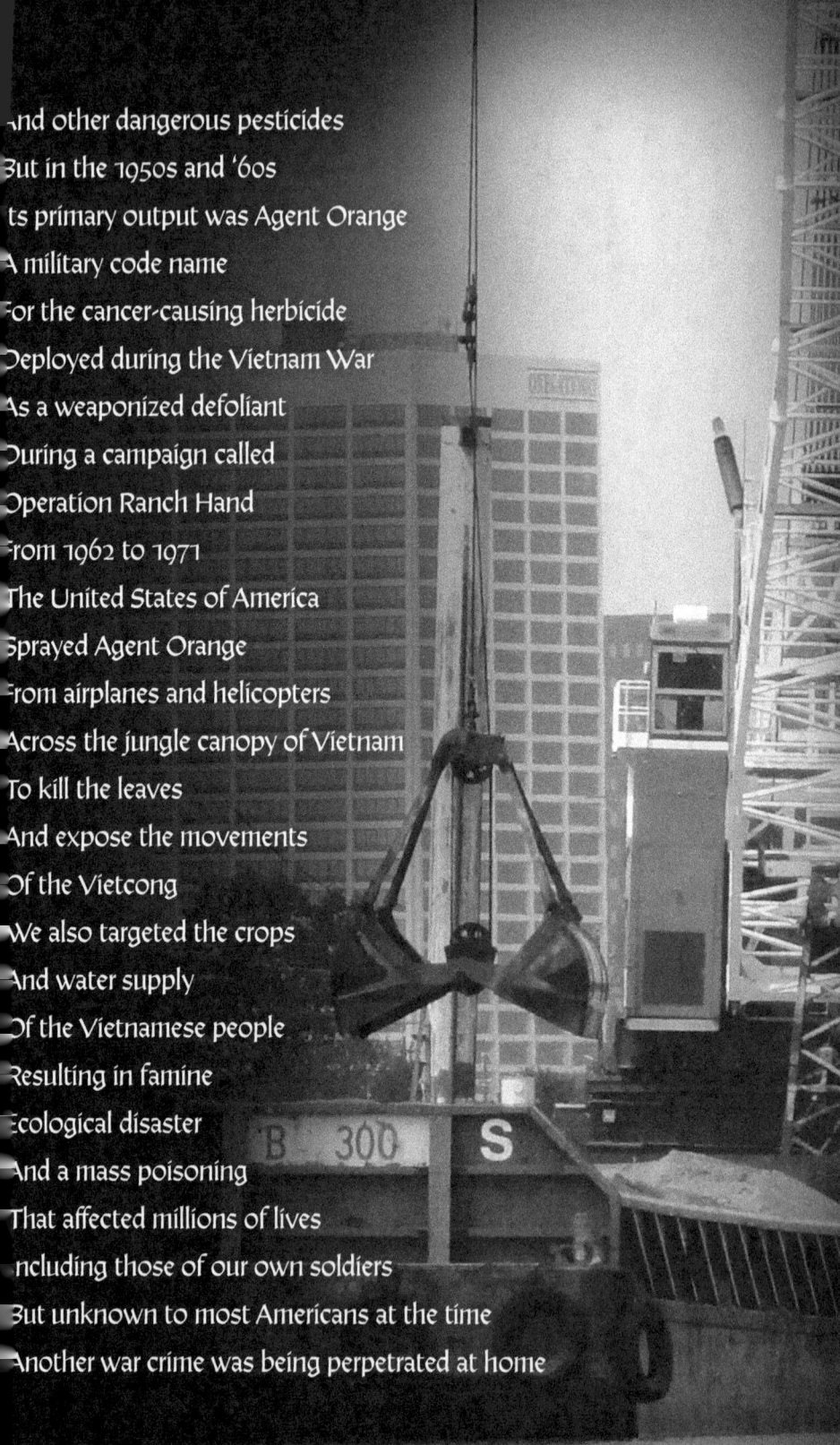

And other dangerous pesticides
But in the 1950s and '60s
Its primary output was Agent Orange
A military code name
For the cancer-causing herbicide
Deployed during the Vietnam War
As a weaponized defoliant
During a campaign called
Operation Ranch Hand
From 1962 to 1971
The United States of America
Sprayed Agent Orange
From airplanes and helicopters
Across the jungle canopy of Vietnam
To kill the leaves
And expose the movements
Of the Vietcong
We also targeted the crops
And water supply
Of the Vietnamese people
Resulting in famine
Ecological disaster
And a mass poisoning
That affected millions of lives
Including those of our own soldiers
But unknown to most Americans at the time
Another war crime was being perpetrated at home

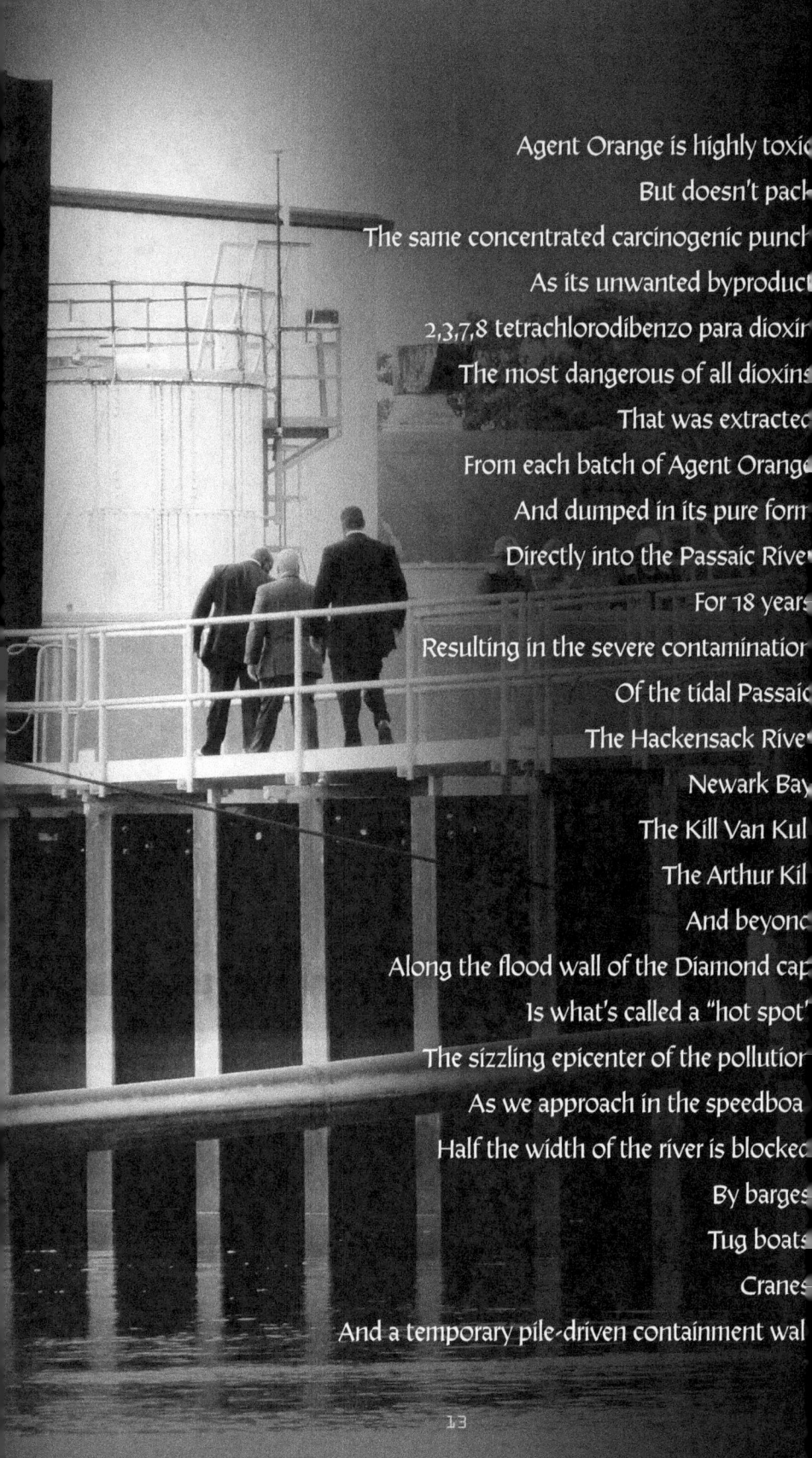

Agent Orange is highly toxic
But doesn't pack
The same concentrated carcinogenic punch
As its unwanted byproduct
2,3,7,8 tetrachlorodibenzo para dioxin
The most dangerous of all dioxins
That was extracted
From each batch of Agent Orange
And dumped in its pure form
Directly into the Passaic River
For 18 years
Resulting in the severe contamination
Of the tidal Passaic
The Hackensack River
Newark Bay
The Kill Van Kull
The Arthur Kill
And beyond
Along the flood wall of the Diamond cap
Is what's called a "hot spot"
The sizzling epicenter of the pollution
As we approach in the speedboat
Half the width of the river is blocked
By barges
Tug boats
Cranes
And a temporary pile-driven containment wall

Giant corrugated pieces of interlocking steel

That form a box around the dredge area

To prevent plumes of dioxin sediment

From spreading any further while they dig

We've been watching these guys

So we know

That usually the crane would be busy at this time of day

Dumping bucket after bucket of toxic mud

Into a listing barge

But for some reason the dredging is stopped

No black smoke belching from the stack

No workers on the decks

I cut the speed to reduce our wake

And just then we spot a man

Standing on the crane barge

Wearing a suit

Leaning over the railing

He's looking at something

And my wife and I correctly surmise

At exactly the same time

That the workers must have found:

"A dead body!"

More suits appear as we get closer

And the Prosecutor's Mobile Command Unit

Comes into view

Parked on the Superfund cap

Then we see the State Police boat

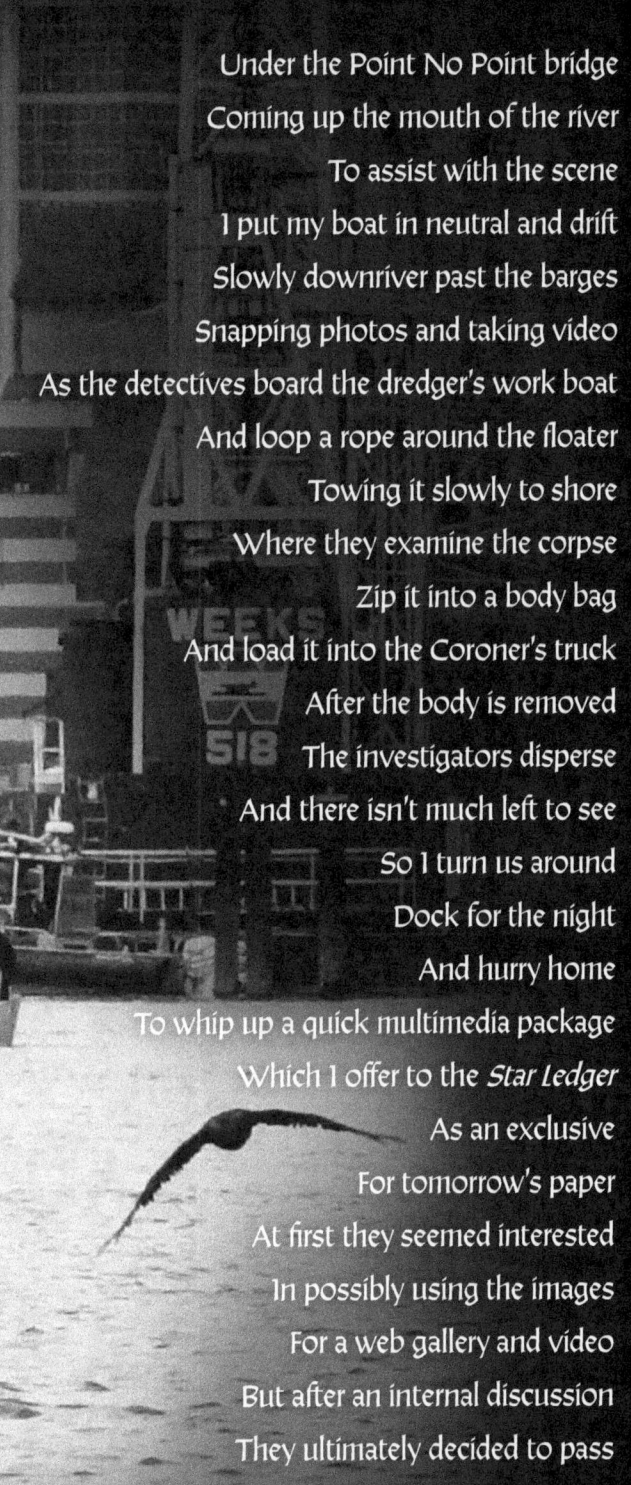

Under the Point No Point bridge
Coming up the mouth of the river
To assist with the scene
I put my boat in neutral and drift
Slowly downriver past the barges
Snapping photos and taking video
As the detectives board the dredger's work boat
And loop a rope around the floater
Towing it slowly to shore
Where they examine the corpse
Zip it into a body bag
And load it into the Coroner's truck
After the body is removed
The investigators disperse
And there isn't much left to see
So I turn us around
Dock for the night
And hurry home
To whip up a quick multimedia package
Which I offer to the *Star Ledger*
As an exclusive
For tomorrow's paper
At first they seemed interested
In possibly using the images
For a web gallery and video
But after an internal discussion
They ultimately decided to pass

The next day a small blurb

With three lines of text

Appeared on nj.com

Featuring only a thumbnail map of Newark

Instead of a picture

I felt a little sad for the unnamed dead man

Whose passing generated so few waves

But I know it's not the *Star Ledger*'s fault

That's just the way life goes in the Ironbound

Floaters are so common

On this river of death

They're barely even newsworthy

I can only guess what was said

During the staff meeting

But I can almost see the editors

Reviewing the images

As they shrug their shoulders and figure:

Just another corpse in the Passaic

No big deal...

Happens all the time

# # #

VOODOO RIVER

One summer afternoo
At the Nutley boat ram
A splash of unusual colo
In the underbrusl
Caught my ey
Upon closer inspectior
I discoverec
Two aluminum oven trays
Turkey-sized pans
Placed haphazardly
On the riverbank
And filled to the brim
With weird stuff:
Cap guns
Mouse traps
Lollipops
Burnt cigars

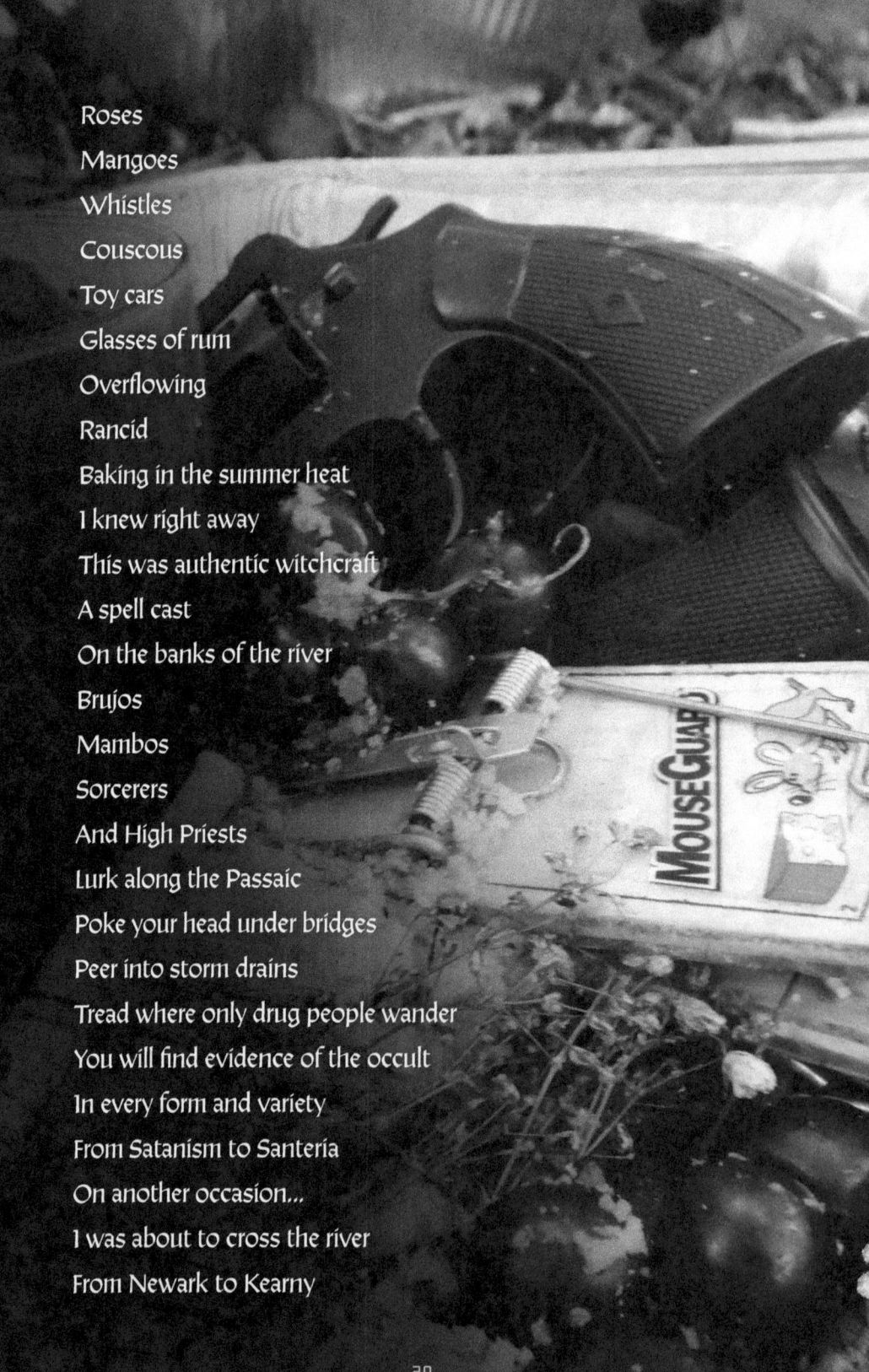

Roses

Mangoes

Whistles

Couscous

Toy cars

Glasses of rum

Overflowing

Rancid

Baking in the summer heat

I knew right away

This was authentic witchcraft

A spell cast

On the banks of the river

Brujos

Mambos

Sorcerers

And High Priests

Lurk along the Passaic

Poke your head under bridges

Peer into storm drains

Tread where only drug people wander

You will find evidence of the occult

In every form and variety

From Satanism to Santería

On another occasion...

I was about to cross the river

From Newark to Kearny

On the abandoned railroad bridge
Known locally as *The Cut*
When I happened upon a calabash bowl
Fifty feet above the Passaic
Containing a decapitated rooster
Burnt photographs
Half-smoked cigars
And something resembling a squashed tomato
That may or may not have been
A disembodied animal heart
The sacrifice rested on a veritable altar
Of used hypodermic needles
Meanwhile upstream...
On the Clifton/Garfield border
Below the Dundee Dam
Two fishermen spot an unusual bag
Floating down the Passaic River
They wade out and grab it
Only to discover the tiny cadaver
Of a two-year-old girl
Shrouded in plastic
Still wearing a hospice wristband
Turns out she was gravenapped
From 50 miles away
In Stamford, Connecticut
Dead for two years
But remarkably preserved

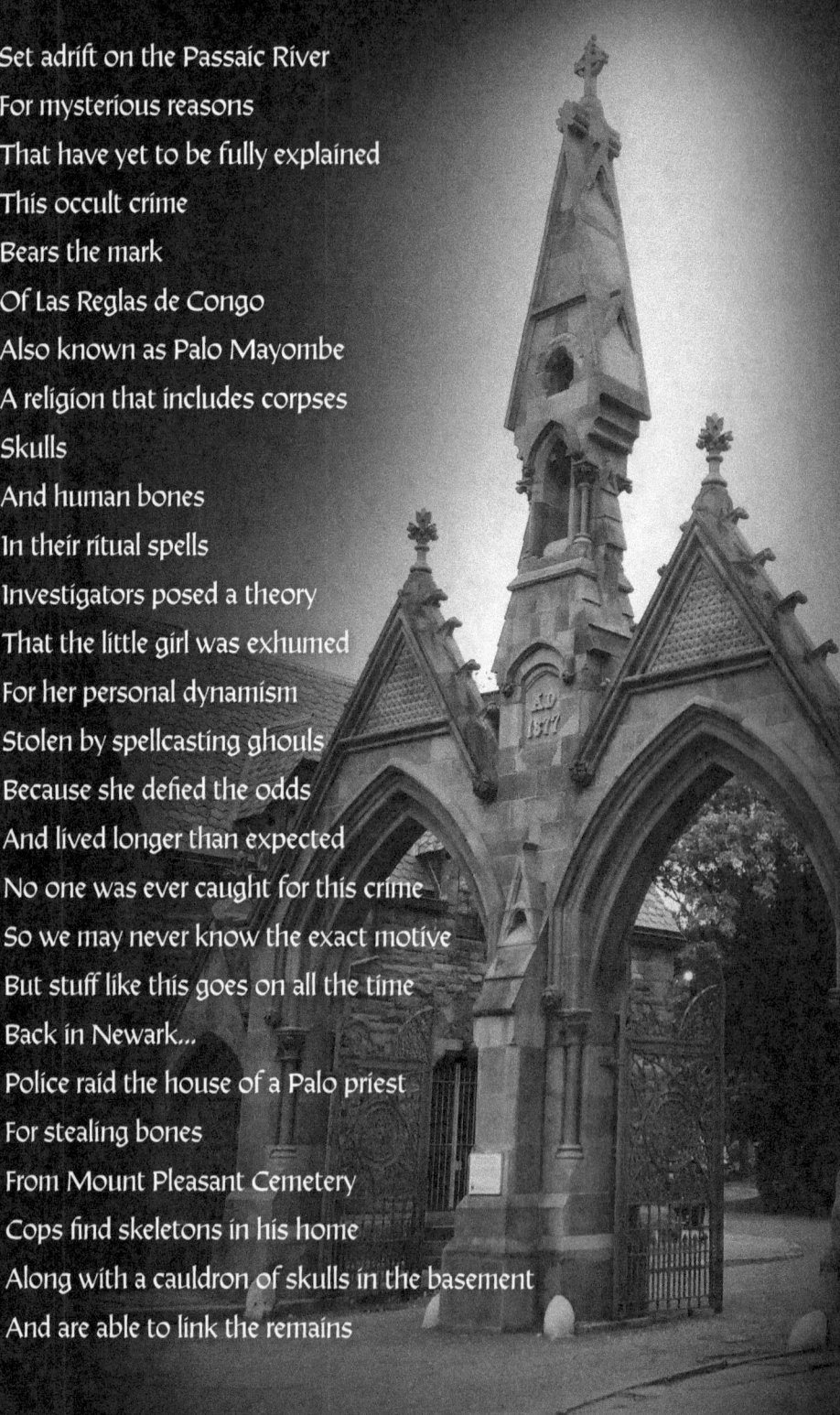

Set adrift on the Passaic River
For mysterious reasons
That have yet to be fully explained
This occult crime
Bears the mark
Of Las Reglas de Congo
Also known as Palo Mayombe
A religion that includes corpses
Skulls
And human bones
In their ritual spells
Investigators posed a theory
That the little girl was exhumed
For her personal dynamism
Stolen by spellcasting ghouls
Because she defied the odds
And lived longer than expected
No one was ever caught for this crime
So we may never know the exact motive
But stuff like this goes on all the time
Back in Newark...
Police raid the house of a Palo priest
For stealing bones
From Mount Pleasant Cemetery
Cops find skeletons in his home
Along with a cauldron of skulls in the basement
And are able to link the remains

To desecrated grave sites
The priest received a five-year sentence
But he's out by now
Ritual sacrifices happen nightly
In North Jersey
We paved the marsh
And walled the river
But the human swamps
Of our sprawling cities
Still teem with mystery
Whenever I wander the shoreline
Or explore in the boat
I always keep a lookout
For magick along the Passaic

\# \# \#

OUR FIRST PADDLE

Back in 2005
I had the overwhelming urge to own a boat
I kept seeing wetlands
Out my car window
That I yearned to explore
So I bought an old fiberglass canoe
Painted her flat black
And christened her *Nightshade*
My daughter is all grown up now
But on the day of our first voyage
She was seven
I lashed the *Nightshade* to the roof of the car
Belted Star into her booster seat
And drove up Route 287
To the White Bridge Launch
For a test paddle
Through the Great Swamp

After setting our gear on the bank
I adjusted Star's life preserver
Got her comfortable in the bow
And shoved us out
Onto the glittering Passaic River
The canoe handling wonderfully
Carrying us along a watery path
Of lily pads
Cattails
Jumping fish
And great blue heron
At some point Star asked:
"Are we still in New Jersey?"
And it was a valid question
This healthy forest
Doesn't resemble
The chaotic suburbs
Where we normally dwell
The Great Swamp is vibrant and alive
As the river meanders through grasslands
Shady woods
And fields of wildflowers
To discover the shallow headwaters
Of the Passaic River
Is to find peace
And this tranquility drew us back
On many future expeditions

To the White Bridge launch
Even as the river
Occasionally shifted course
We were present
To watch the changes
And evolve
Into the adults we became
But I can still see us paddling on that first day
Star as a seven-year-old kid
Me as a 28-year-old dad
Growing up together
On the Passaic
Sharing treasured adventures
That will never fade
No matter where the river takes us

# # #

SHARKEY'S DUMP

Part 1: Getting there

The Pio Costa industrial complex
In Fairfield, New Jersey
Is a good place to launch the *Nightshade*
When I want to take the long way
To the capped mounds of Sharkey's Dump
I have a two-stroke outboard
That basically transforms the canoe
Into a moped for the water
The engine is only 1.5 horsepower
But does the job
As I pass under the Pine Brook Bridge
And head upstream on the Passaic River
It's so much fun to cruise around back here
Motoring through the forest

Where trees lean over the river

From both banks

Their branches touching overhead

Arching into a green canopy

That forms a tunnel through the swamp

There are many tributaries in this area

Joining forces with the Passaic

I know I'm getting close to the Rockaway River

When the water beneath the canoe

Starts to whirl and spin

Along the left shore the current is murky brown

While water on the right bank

Pours crystal clear from the Rockaway

Into the rich chocolate milk

Of the Passaic

Both rivers blend midstream

Creating swirling vortexes

Of coffee creamer tornadoes

That break off into psychedelic fractals

And spin past the boat

I swing the bow of the canoe starboard

Taking the right fork

Straight up the mouth of the Rockaway

Where I ease back on the gas

And go a little slower on this small tributary

With its slalom course of snags

Fallen trees

And submerged boulders
Somehow managing
To make it past these obstacles
Without breaking the shear pin on the propeller
I emerge from the thick forest
And find the confluence
Of the Whippany and Rockaway rivers
Which is also the location
Of a sewage treatment plant
Where the toilets of over 50,000 people
From Parsippany-Troy Hills
Are flushed into one central location
Which explains the excrement I've been smelling
For the past half-mile or so
A dark brown smell
Wafting from vast pools of human waste
Reeking like death in the throbbing sun
This evil odor is relatively new
And was unknown to the natives
Back when this was a Lenape paradise
And the rivers had pure Algonquian names
Before the fecal pipes
Power lines
Toxic waste
And carbon-belching highways invaded the wetlands
Before the army of plastic bottles
Assembled their ranks in the swamps

The indigenous people named these watercourses:

Pahsayek

Reckowacky

Whippanong

And the rivers were clean

But no more

The swamp is now deeply toxic

And in addition to the pollution

The canoeing gets a little sketchy here as well

I wanted to get further up the Rockaway

But the river is narrow for a spell

Creating a strong current

That impedes my progress

I hop out and drag the *Nightshade*

Through thick underbrush

To an eddy above the swift water

Where I relaunch the canoe

Put fresh gas in the outboard

And get her cranking again

To glide through plumes of duckweed

Heading upstream on the Rockaway

Toward the capped mounds of Sharkey's Dump

Part 2: UFO Sighting

Back in the 1930s
There was an enormous pig farm
On the swampy land
Where the Rockaway
And Whippany rivers converge
Somewhere around 1945
The pig farm transitioned into a disposal area
Known as Sharkey Landfill
Or in local vernacular "Sharkey's Dump"
Trucks tipped trash here for 27 years
Forming islands of garbage
That choked the Rockaway River

By the early 1970s
The landfill was sprawling out of control
And had to be shut down
Which led to the discovery
Of illegally dumped toxic waste
On a truly apocalyptic scale
By the time the EPA got involved
Sharkey's was a chemical death zone

Toluene

Benzene

Chloroform

Acetone

Cyanide

Mercury

Cadmium

Lead

Xylene

Pyrene

Methylnaphthalene

Were detected by the ton
In the groundwater and soil
To combat the spread of this pollution
The government built two massive caps
That cover the main fill sites
One of these caps is a 26-acre island
Located right smack dab
In the middle of the Rockaway River

The toxins under the cap were not removed
They were entombed
Beneath a pile of engineered stone
That rises from the water
Like a multilayered scab
And this is my destination today
So I continue up the Rockaway
Stash the canoe on the far side of the island
Scramble up the steep slope
And sit for awhile on the summit
Catching my breath
And while I'm perched up here on the capstone
I think back to another time
Many summers ago
When I snuck onto this property with a girlfriend
For an evening at Sharkey's Dump
And we sat on these same rocks
Watching the sunset
Until just after nightfall
When we spotted the first UFO
At first we thought it was an airplane
With a single red light
Flying fast and low over Troy Meadows
It looked like the craft was coming right towards us
We even braced for it
Expecting to feel a whoosh over our heads
But it suddenly changed course without slowing or banking

Pinballing off to the south at high speeds

We didn't have long to wait

Before an identical aircraft came into view

Following the same flightpath

Easily tracked by its unblinking red light

It reached the invisible point in the sky

And abruptly changed direction

In an eerie display of airmanship

That blatantly defied the laws of physics

By the time the third UFO appeared

We were on our feet

Staring at the red light in amazement

Watching the ship come in

Just like the first two

Low and fast

Making absolutely zero noise

It came to the prearranged point in the sky

And shot off due south

Racing toward the horizon in a blur of speed

After the third aircraft was gone from view

The show was over for the night

But reflecting back on that evening

From this sunny landfill afternoon

Our close encounter doesn't seem far fetched

Because now I know

From my travels on the Passaic River

That there are strange things in the swamp

Hidden from society
By a shallow stream of water
Mysterious oddities
Waiting to be discovered
By anyone with a canoe
And an intrepid spirit
The land here is tainted
The water is poisoned
And the air smells like shit
But if you want to witness some UFOs
Sharkey's Dump is a damn fine place to visit

\# \# \#

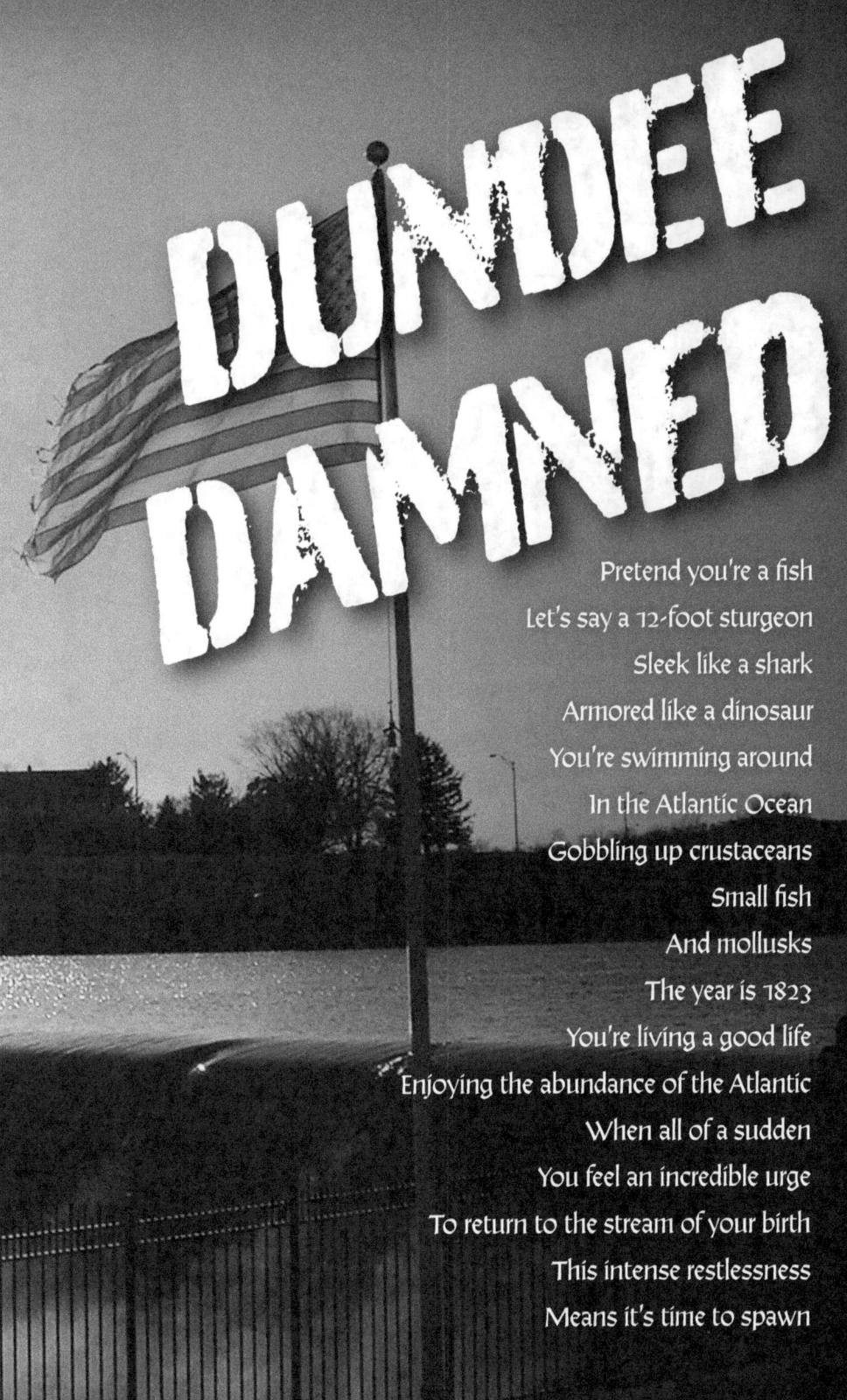

DUNDEE
DAMNED

Pretend you're a fish
Let's say a 12-foot sturgeon
Sleek like a shark
Armored like a dinosaur
You're swimming around
In the Atlantic Ocean
Gobbling up crustaceans
Small fish
And mollusks
The year is 1823
You're living a good life
Enjoying the abundance of the Atlantic
When all of a sudden
You feel an incredible urge
To return to the stream of your birth
This intense restlessness
Means it's time to spawn

So you swim past Sandy Hook

Through Raritan Bay

Up the Arthur Kill

Past Staten Island

You travel the entire length of Newark Bay

And up the mouth of the Passaic River

You swim for another 25 miles

Through brackish waters

Until you reach the base of the Great Falls

In Paterson, New Jersey

Where you find all your friends and relatives

Gathered for the spring spawn

Revved up and ready to party

This is the place of your birth

A lush paradise below the Great Falls

Containing the perfect combination of factors

That will allow you to successfully reproduce

Sounds great doesn't it?

Like a veritable Garden of Eden

But unfortunately for your offspring

They happen to be born in the year 1823

Which means by the time they mature

And feel their own urge to reproduce

It will be too late

Because the spawning party ends in 1833

When humans erect the Dundee Dam

Between Garfield and Clifton, New Jersey

Condemning any sturgeon born after that time

To never return

Severing the essential life cycle

By completely blocking the river

And effectively ending upstream fish migration

This crime against nature

Might have been justified

If the dam served some essential purpose

But get this:

The dam was built to divert water

Into a man-made waterway called the Dundee Canal

The Dundee Canal was built

So boat traffic could continue past the dam

Which is an insane example of circular logic

That begs the question:

Why build a dam in the first place

If all you want to do is go around it?

The canal was ill conceived

Wasteful from the start

And didn't end well

Upon completion

The 7.8 mile Dundee Canal

Was used only one time

By one single barge

Before it was deemed obsolete

Unnecessary

And classified as a complete financial failure

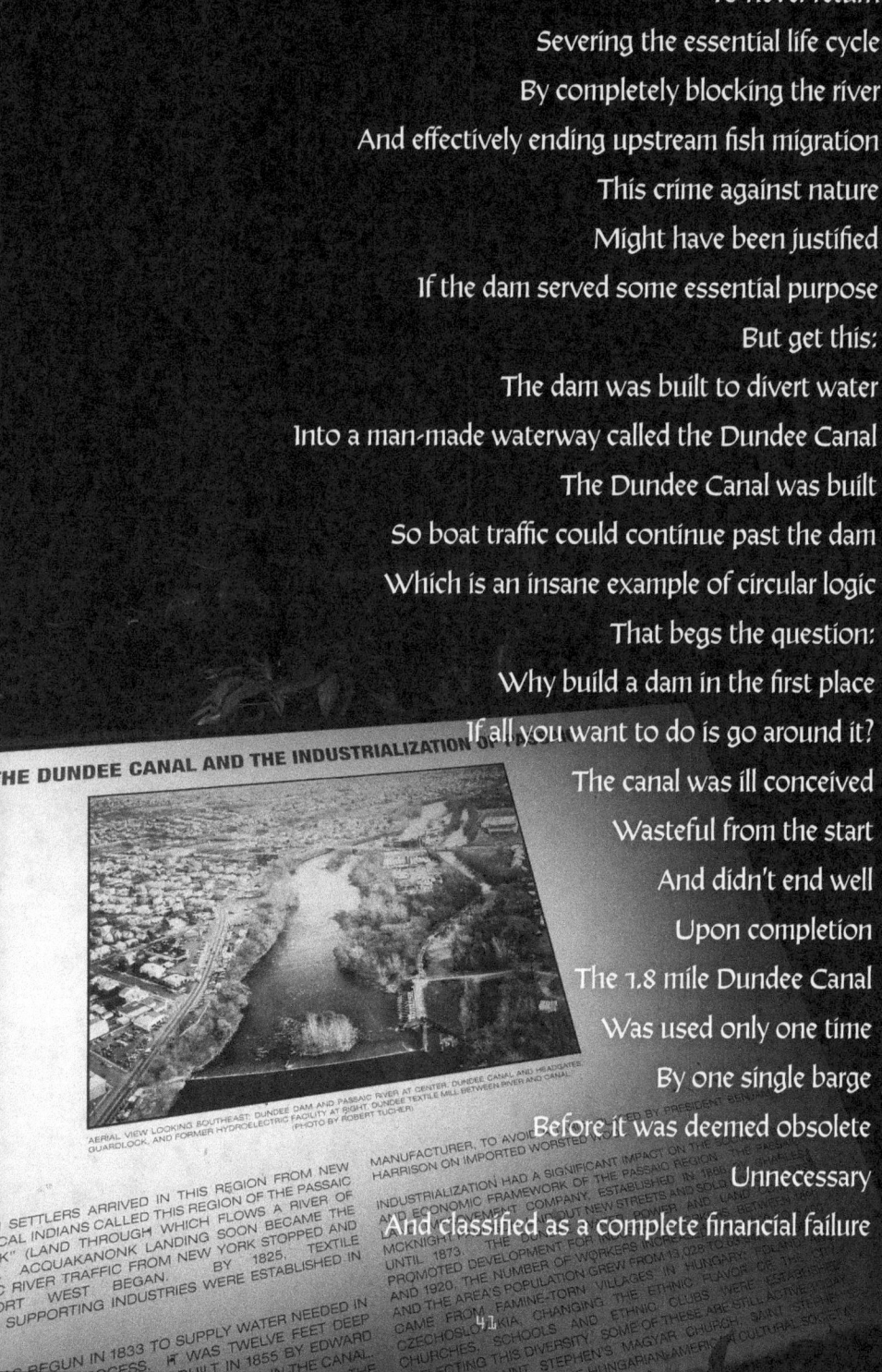

THE DUNDEE CANAL AND THE INDUSTRIALIZATION OF ...

"AERIAL VIEW LOOKING SOUTHEAST: DUNDEE DAM AND PASSAIC RIVER AT CENTER, DUNDEE CANAL AND HEADGATES,
GUARDLOCK, AND FORMER HYDROELECTRIC FACILITY AT RIGHT, DUNDEE TEXTILE MILL BETWEEN RIVER AND CANAL.
(PHOTO BY ROBERT TUCHER)

41

It was such a bad piece of business

That it drove the Dundee Manufacturing Company

To bankruptcy and collapse

But even though the canal was a flop

And the dam caused the extermination

Of several species

A diverted Passaic River happened to be useful

For generating hydroelectric power

So the Dundee Dam stayed

And still stands to this day

Despite the fact that it's structurally unsound

And doesn't even provide hydro power anymore

The massive stone wall stretches across the Passaic

Preventing access to ancient spawning grounds

Where mammoth sturgeon like yourself

Once frolicked by the hundreds of thousands

Where herring laid eggs by the millions

Where infinite numbers of shad

Found collective climax

After their long journey from the sea

But this paradise is lost

The dam disrupted ancient breeding rituals

Destroyed countless generations of fish

And permanently transformed the upstream river

Into a fetid pond known as Dundee Lake

A stretch of the Passaic that stews and bubbles

In a murky brown miasma of toxic mud

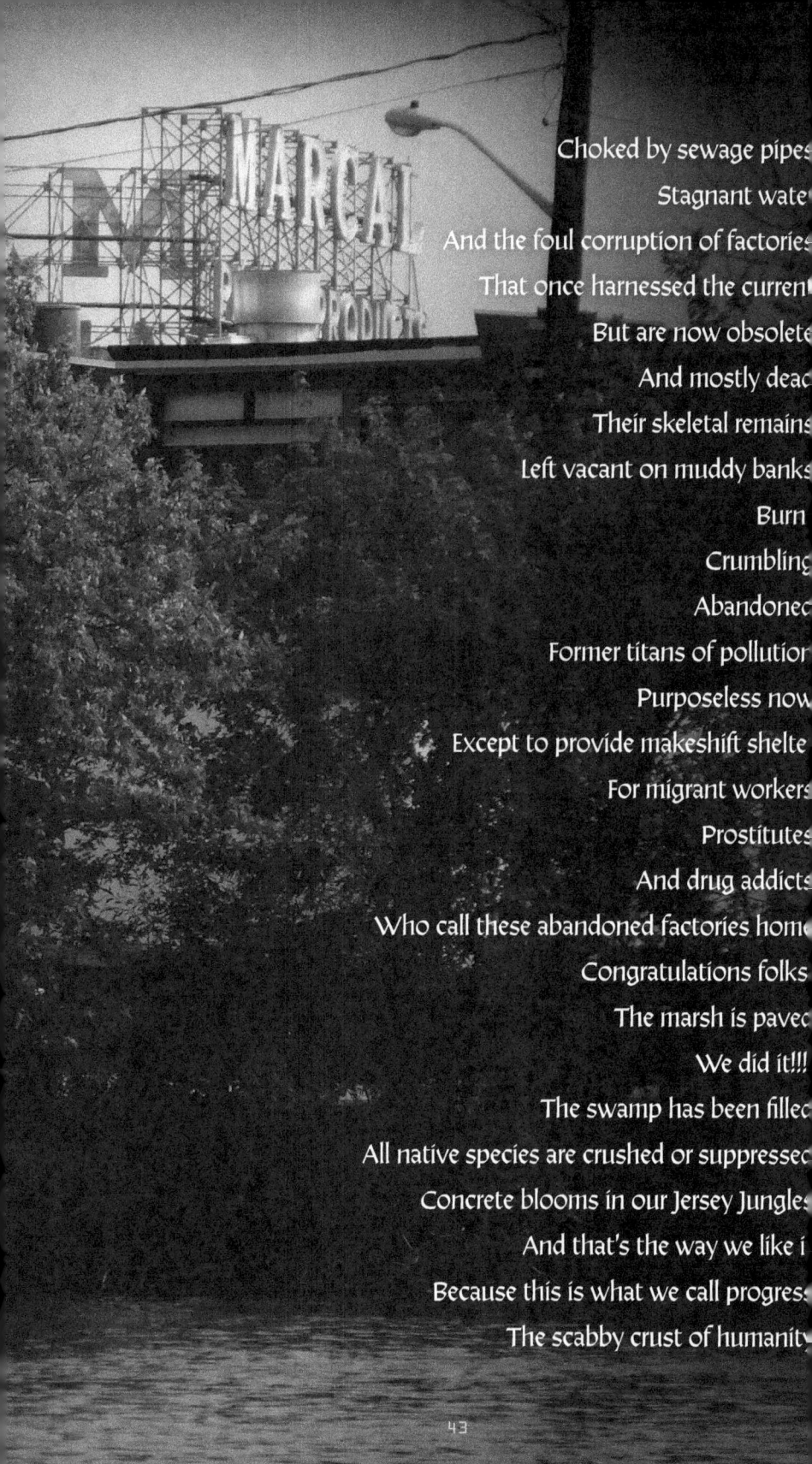

Choked by sewage pipes
Stagnant water
And the foul corruption of factories
That once harnessed the current
But are now obsolete
And mostly dead
Their skeletal remains
Left vacant on muddy banks
Burn
Crumbling
Abandoned
Former titans of pollution
Purposeless now
Except to provide makeshift shelter
For migrant workers
Prostitutes
And drug addicts
Who call these abandoned factories home
Congratulations folks
The marsh is paved
We did it!!!
The swamp has been filled
All native species are crushed or suppressed
Concrete blooms in our Jersey Jungles
And that's the way we like it
Because this is what we call progress
The scabby crust of humanity

Hardening across the landscape
The lust in our hearts
Dooming us to grow
And grow
And grow
Until we are so overpopulated
That we crush our habitat
Beneath the stamp of our civilization
And somehow we're always surprised
When the water rises
We're shocked
When the river backs up behind our dams
Flows into our streets
And enters our homes
Sometimes years will go by without a flood
And we forget about the Passaic
We keep tearing down trees
And building up wetlands
With our relentless development
Thinking we're so clever
Until the skies open up
The waters surge
And the cleanup bill rises into the multi-billions
The swamps were once a vast basin
A squishy sponge eager to soak up water
When the floods came
The river crested harmlessly

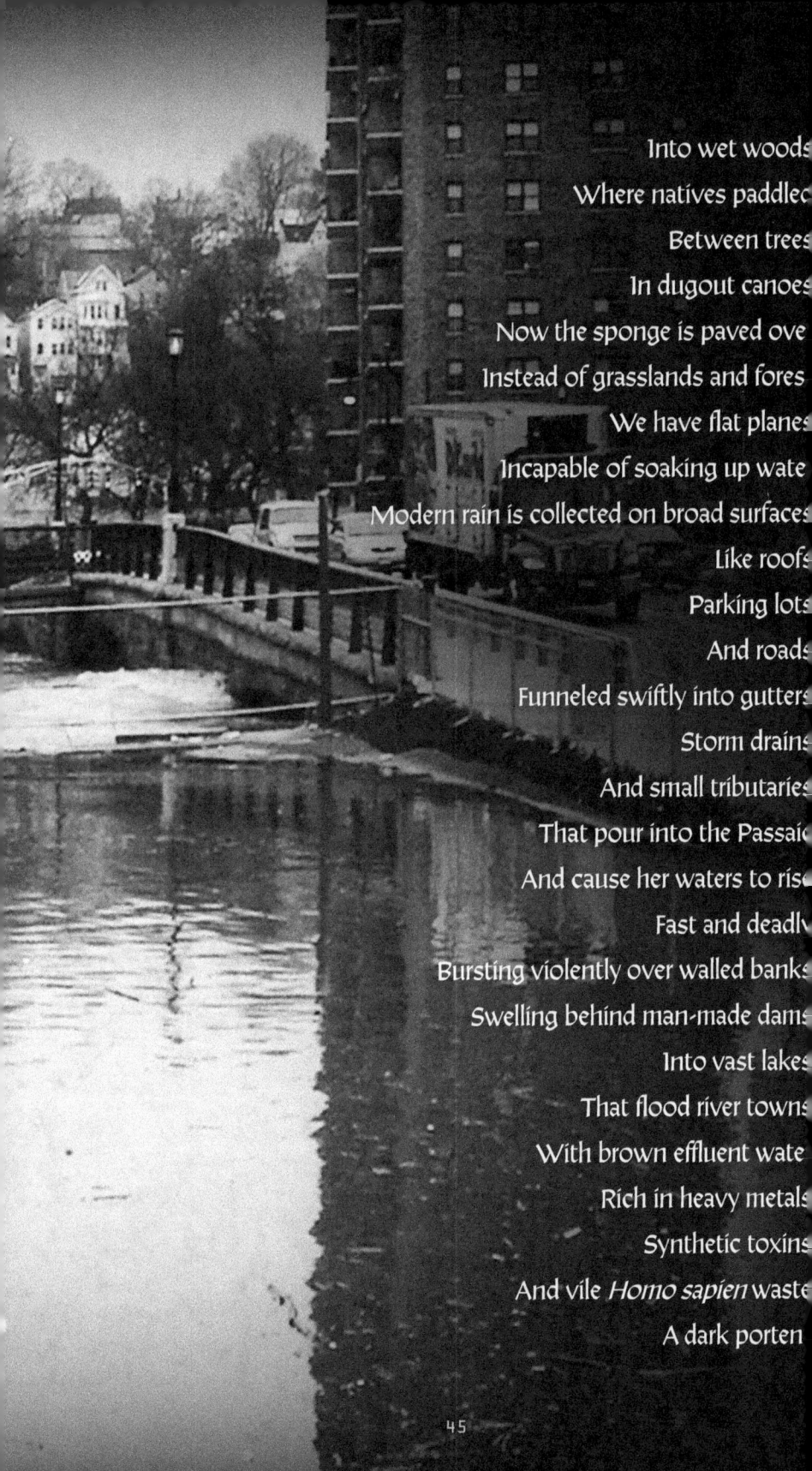

Into wet woods

Where natives paddled

Between trees

In dugout canoes

Now the sponge is paved ove

Instead of grasslands and fores

We have flat planes

Incapable of soaking up wate

Modern rain is collected on broad surfaces

Like roofs

Parking lots

And roads

Funneled swiftly into gutters

Storm drains

And small tributaries

That pour into the Passaic

And cause her waters to rise

Fast and deadly

Bursting violently over walled banks

Swelling behind man-made dams

Into vast lakes

That flood river towns

With brown effluent wate

Rich in heavy metals

Synthetic toxins

And vile *Homo sapien* waste

A dark porten

Of a very bleak future

For the swamp

For the wildlife

And for humanity

Look at your surroundings people!

It's already too late

New Jersey will surely sink itself

Along with the rest of the planet

And there will be no safe place left

In the whole wide world

For a 12-foot sturgeon like you

Anymore

# # #

ANNIE'S ROAD

If you're from North Jersey
There is a very good chance
That you're already familiar with Annie's Road
I cruise this stretch on a regular basis
To get from Paterson to Little Falls
Where the two-lane blacktop
Twists and turns through Totowa
Along a steeply wooded hill
That overlooks the Passaic River
Maps list this thoroughfare as "Riverview Drive"
But locals mostly call it "Annie's Road"
A term I never properly understood
Until I read about Annie
In the pages of *Weird NJ* magazine
Like most urban legends
There are many variations to the myth

The earliest fables I've heard about Annie
Date back to the 1700s
And take place during colonial times
These tales usually describe Annie
As a young bride-to-be
Walking with her family down Riverview Drive
Toward a shady glen by the river
Where her groom is eagerly waiting
It's the happiest day of Annie's life
But just as her fiance comes within sight
A runaway horse carriage whips around a bend
Slams into Annie from behind
And drags her beneath the rear axle
For several hundred yards
Until her body is flung clear
And her corpse lands with a thud
At the feet of her horrified fiance
A more contemporary version
Of the Annie's Road legend
Takes place in the 1960s
This time Annie is cast as an angry prom queen
Who gets into an argument with her date
Storms out of the dance
And decides to walk home
As she is plodding along in high heels
On the narrow shoulder of Riverview Drive
A truck comes around the bend

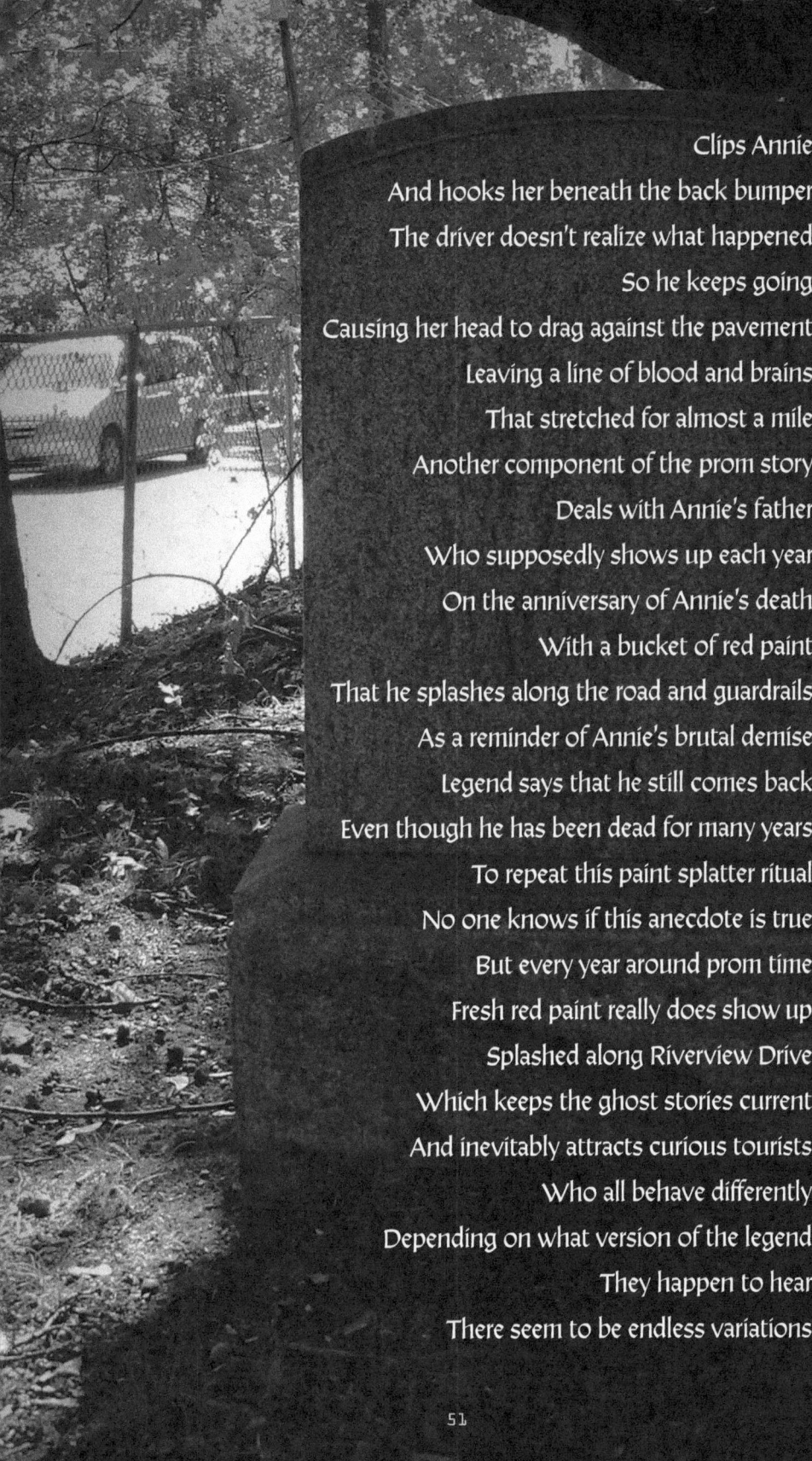

Clips Annie

And hooks her beneath the back bumper

The driver doesn't realize what happened

So he keeps going

Causing her head to drag against the pavement

Leaving a line of blood and brains

That stretched for almost a mile

Another component of the prom story

Deals with Annie's father

Who supposedly shows up each year

On the anniversary of Annie's death

With a bucket of red paint

That he splashes along the road and guardrails

As a reminder of Annie's brutal demise

Legend says that he still comes back

Even though he has been dead for many years

To repeat this paint splatter ritual

No one knows if this anecdote is true

But every year around prom time

Fresh red paint really does show up

Splashed along Riverview Drive

Which keeps the ghost stories current

And inevitably attracts curious tourists

Who all behave differently

Depending on what version of the legend

They happen to hear

There seem to be endless variations

Circulating around at any given time
Annie's story is just as popular at the local bar
As it is in the neighborhood schools
Everyone around here knows about Annie's Road
And each time the story is told it changes a little bit
The details depend on who is spinning the yarn
Most narrators are somewhat merciful in the telling
Sticking with the vehicular dragging theme
Which is a relatively quick death
But sometimes Annie dies in more sadistic ways
One particularly sinister variant of the prom story
Has Annie leaving the dance on foot
Only to be abducted by a van full of necrophiles
Who beat Annie to death
Rape her lifeless body
And toss her defiled corpse over the guardrail
Where it slides down the muddy bank
And into the Passaic River
Only a sicko would go there with the story
But no matter which scenario you hear
It will always conclude
With Annie as a ghost
Haunting Riverview Drive in a long white dress
Appearing suddenly in front of cars
Forcing drivers to swerve into the trees
And die themselves
Along Annie's Road

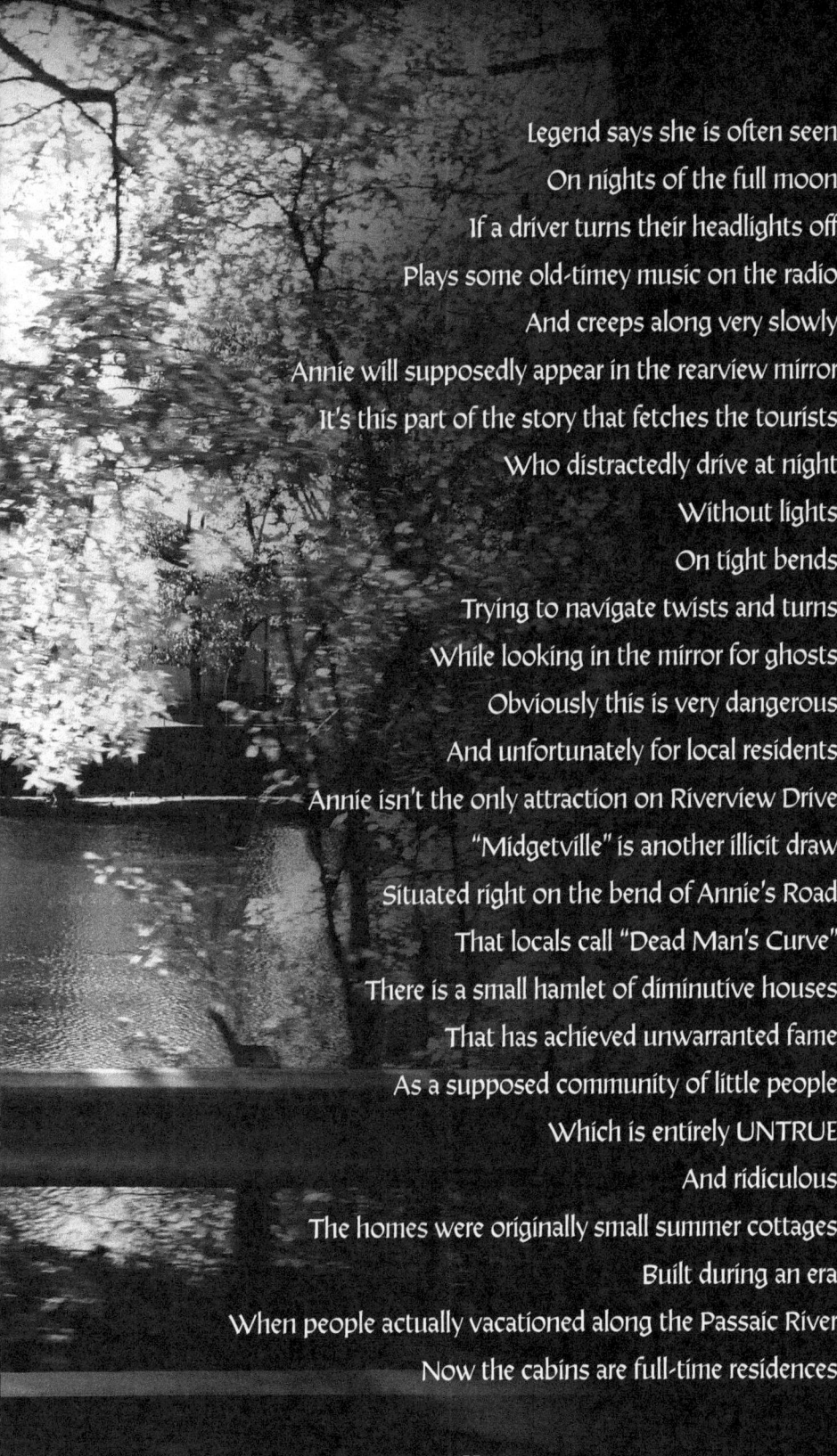

Legend says she is often seen

On nights of the full moon

If a driver turns their headlights off

Plays some old-timey music on the radio

And creeps along very slowly

Annie will supposedly appear in the rearview mirror

It's this part of the story that fetches the tourists

Who distractedly drive at night

Without lights

On tight bends

Trying to navigate twists and turns

While looking in the mirror for ghosts

Obviously this is very dangerous

And unfortunately for local residents

Annie isn't the only attraction on Riverview Drive

"Midgetville" is another illicit draw

Situated right on the bend of Annie's Road

That locals call "Dead Man's Curve"

There is a small hamlet of diminutive houses

That has achieved unwarranted fame

As a supposed community of little people

Which is entirely UNTRUE

And ridiculous

The homes were originally small summer cottages

Built during an era

When people actually vacationed along the Passaic River

Now the cabins are full-time residences

Where perfectly normal-sized people dwell
Unfounded rumors about "midgets"
(A horribly offensive term by the way)
Are nothing but urban legend
Pure kids stuff and nonsense
The fact that only average-size people live there
Is well documented
But even if there were little people living in "Midgetville"
Why would anyone think it's OK to harass them?
Here's the usual scenario:
People come to Annie's Road hoping to see a ghost
When Annie inevitably fails to appear
"Midgetville" serves as a supplemental adventure
Usually leading to interactions with the locals
Which rarely go well
Though the residents of "Midgetville" are not dwarfs
They *are* extremely angry
And for good reason
Because they have been terrorized
Hassled
And assaulted
By loud
Obnoxious
Sightseers
Showing up drunk
Outside their houses at night
Honking horns

Throwing eggs

Screaming for the "midgets" to show themselves

In one such incident

A kid got into an altercation with a resident

And shot him in the head with a frozen paintball

Cracking the poor guy's skull

And almost killing him

For absolutely no good reason at all

After this senseless assault

The police got more serious about patrolling

Hung a bunch of warning signs

And created a roadblock at one end of the neighborhood

But the preventive measures

Haven't stopped the ghost hunters

Joy riders

Curiosity seekers

And packs of nocturnal teenagers

Who seek out the backwaters of North Jersey

In search of "Midgets"

Dwarfs

And the restless woman in white

Of Annie's Road

# # #

BLAZING THROUGH THE SWAMP

For two seasons I cruised the lower Passaic
In the *Sevas Natas*
My 17-foot fiberglass speed boat
Painted flat black with skull and crossbones
And a 70-horsepower outboard
The expedition was of a literary nature
To write a book called *Wheeler on the Passaic*
Headquarters was Rapp's Boatyard
The last working marina on the Passaic River
Located on the muddy banks of Kearny, New Jersey
Where I rented a boat slip from 2012-2013
Hurricane Sandy hit NJ hard in the fall of 2012
Almost wiped the boatyard off the map
The nine-foot storm surge decimated Rapp's
Sloshing five feet of stormwater into the machine shop

Completely wrecking the yard

Picking up boats from storage

Shifting them off their blocks

And in some cases carrying them away downriver

The *Sevas Natas* was safe in Montclair during the storm

But the boatyard was so completely trashed

That the prospect of a 2013 boating season looked grim

It took a lot of hard work to get Rapp's even semi-usable

I cleared a path to the docks

Cleaned up the shop as best I could

And repaired the stairs so Mr. Rapp could get inside

Conditions were less than ideal

But Mr. Rapp agreed to let me keep my slip

And we persisted for one final boating season

Amongst the wreckage

Spring

Summer

Fall

The *Sevas Natas* patrolled

The lower Passaic River

Newark Bay

And the lower Hack

While I wrote it all down in my journal

Eventually filling six composition notebooks

With adventure stories from the Passaic River

Docking a boat on this heavily polluted waterway

With its temperamental tides and harsh urban vibe

Would put serious pressure on any vessel
But was especially tough on my 1973 Glastron
And her 1985 70-horsepower Evinrude
One hot summer day
Shortly after casting off from Rapp's
The outboard overheated a mile downstream
I killed the engine as steam billowed from the stern
And tied up to the pilings of the NX Bridge
Where I waited about an hour for the motor to cool
Eventually limping back to the dock at Rapp's
With the boat at the slowest speed possible
So as not to boil the engine again
Clearly the outboard needed a new water pump
And for that I was going to need help
My buddy Frank is an auto mechanic by trade
And a Passaic River adventurer by nature
He helped me to find the right boat for this odyssey
And when she breaks down
He always gets her running again
Frank and I pulled the boat out at the Kearny ramp
And towed her back to Frank's Service in Fairfield
Where his friend Tommy stopped by
To assist with the repair job
Tommy is a professional mechanic
And happens to own a 70-hp Evinrude as well
On which he performed an impeller replacement
Just last year

Tommy's expertise was extremely welcome
And there wasn't much for me to do
So I stayed out of the way
And recorded everything with my camera
Here's how the job looks on fast forward:
Tommy removes the propeller
Frank heats the lower unit bolts with a torch
Tommy removes the hot bolts with a hand ratchet
Together they wrestle with the gear case
Eventually getting it disconnected
Tommy carries the lower unit into Frank's garage
And stands it upright by the skeg in a large vice
Frank zips the bolts off the water pump unit
Tommy removes the housing
Together they examine the pump
Confirming that the impeller is indeed cracked
Frank removes the old gaskets
Cleans the flat surfaces with a file
Tommy greases the replacement parts
Together they install the new impeller
Tighten all the bolts
And while they're at it
They decide to change the gear oil in the lower unit
After everything is lubed and connected
They slip the lower unit back in place
Frank greases the threads of the bolts
Tommy hand tightens them in place

After the propeller is reinstalled
The job is complete
So we hook up the outboard to the hose
And start her in the driveway
After a bit of fiddling around
Tommy and Frank have her purring
But we decide to run her under full load
Before sending her back to Kearny
So Frank hitches the trailer to his jeep
And we take a ride to the Passaic River in Fairfield
For a test run through the Great Piece Meadows
Where the river is narrow and serpentine
And can be dangerous for a fast boat
With its sharp turns
Submerged rocks
And sunken logs
Frank owns a particularly quick jet boat
That takes hairpin turns at 40mph
And will snap your head back on a straightaway
He takes this run all the time
So it was natural for him to man the helm
For this test drive through the swamp
As we slid the *Sevas Natas* off the trailer
And proceeded upstream
Into the Great Piece
Once past the houses
Frank jammed on the gas

The motor responding immediately

Eager to go fast

Running perfectly

A nice jet of water pissing out the back

Letting us know the impeller was doing its job

Pumping river water through the outboard

Expelling the heat

As we came to the first sharp turn

Going about 30 mph

The *Sevas Natas* sent up a huge wake

That rose over the bank of the river

And crashed into the woods like a tsunami

We were frighteningly close to the shoreline

And Frank looked at me like

"Phew! Glad we made it"

He is accustomed to driving the jet boat

Which is more maneuverable at high speeds

Than the deep hulled Glastron

But it only took that one close call for Frank to adapt

And from that moment it was on!

He kept the throttle up as far as it would go

And we sped through the Great Piece

Zigging and zagging past obstructions

Whipping around tight bends

Dodging tree branches and rocks

Blasting through the swamp

The river here twists and turns so much

That a boat travels 12 miles
To go four as the crow flies
We made it deep into the bog very quickly
Until a fallen tree
That blocked the entire river
Halted our forward progress
This was as far as we were going to get
So we idled around for awhile
While Tommy made adjustments to the outboard
Tuning it by sound like a musical instrument
Until he found the perfect pitch
And she purred like a kitten
Now it was my turn to drive
I jumped excitedly to the wheel
And instantly we were up
Speeding full throttle with the downstream current
A huge wave of joy fanning out behind me
The forest a green blur in my peripheral vision
Rocketing through the Great Piece
Down the winding tunnel of trees
On a lightning ride of mind-blowing turns
Fabulous near-misses
And absolute freedom
At the wheel of my very own boat
Like all amazing experiences
It was over too fast
As we approached the boat ramp

I slowed us down through the No Wake zone

And we pulled the *Sevas Natas* onto the trailer

I thanked Frank and Tommy for fixing my outboard

And we discussed our mission for the next day

To relaunch the *Sevas Natas*

At the Kearny ramp

So I can patrol the lower river once more

And tell the tale

Of *Wheeler on the Passaic*

# # #

HOME FROM NYC

I took a job with the Amazing Kreskin
An 84-year-old stage mentalist
As his "Road Manager"
Getting him to shows
And appearances
Setting up his performances
Taking photos and video
Updating his web presence
The position only lasted six months
But it was an extremely weird experience
That I wouldn't trade
We flew into Canada during an arctic blast
Attended a wild Horror Con in Atlantic City
And drove through Alligator Alley in the Everglades
Where Kreskin performed his mentalisms
To sold-out audiences
On both Florida coasts
We went to many strange places
But most of the travel was back and forth from NYC

Kreskin's home base is in North Jersey

So depending on traffic

It's usually a hop skip and a jump

To the Playboy Club

The Friars Club

The Fox News studios

Or Manhattan lunch with book publishers

The day I'm thinking of we were down in the East Village

Attending a wake for Vinny Vella

An actor friend of Kreskin's

Best known for his role in The *Sopranos* and *Casino*

We paid our respects to Vinny's family

Grabbed a bite to eat

And headed back to the parking garage

I can still picture it

Late winter on the Lower East Side

Setting sun

Icy wind howling so hard between skyscrapers

That Kreskin almost blew away in the gale

Back in the car

We cruise through the Holland Tunnel

But encounter major traffic in Jersey City

It's the usual clotting of vehicles

Disorganized lines of honking commuters

Extremely tired and cranky

Violently impatient to get home from work

Backed up all the way to suburbia

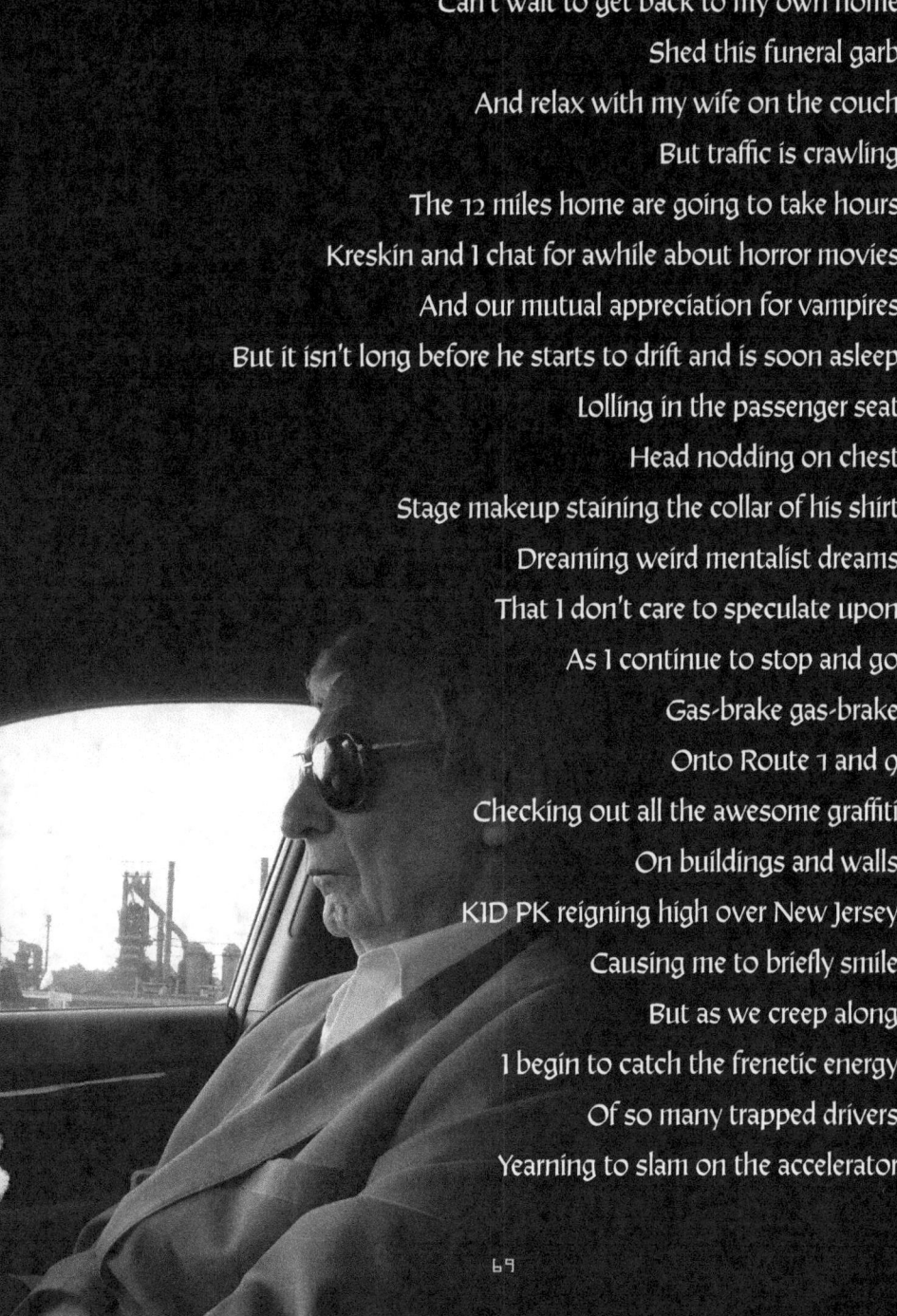

Can't wait to get back to my own home

Shed this funeral garb

And relax with my wife on the couch

But traffic is crawling

The 12 miles home are going to take hours

Kreskin and I chat for awhile about horror movies

And our mutual appreciation for vampires

But it isn't long before he starts to drift and is soon asleep

Lolling in the passenger seat

Head nodding on chest

Stage makeup staining the collar of his shirt

Dreaming weird mentalist dreams

That I don't care to speculate upon

As I continue to stop and go

Gas-brake gas-brake

Onto Route 1 and go

Checking out all the awesome graffiti

On buildings and walls

KID PK reigning high over New Jersey

Causing me to briefly smile

But as we creep along

I begin to catch the frenetic energy

Of so many trapped drivers

Yearning to slam on the accelerator

But stuck stuck stuck

Then we crest the hill on Newark Avenue

Where a panorama of infrastructure suddenly looms

Massive bridges standing erect against the sunset

Silhouettes of steel and concrete

Contrasted across the sun-stained sky

Red

Pink Orange

Yellow

Purple

Blue

Clouds seemingly on fire

Whipping in the roaring wind

And downriver I see them

The five massive stacks

Of the abandoned Kearny Generating Station

And the skeletal dinosaur bones

Of the Pulaski Skyway

A deck truss cantilever masterpiece

With web-works of steel sprouting from statuesque concrete

Delineating between river and sky

All this beauty hits me in one quick glance

But I have plenty of time to gaze

As we inch forward toward the Hackensack River

That gorgeous sister to the Passaic

With her numerous crossings all in one spot

The Path Lift Bridge

The Hack Lift Bridge
The Hack Freight Rail Bridge
The Wittpenn Bridge
And the New Wittpenn Bridge replacement project
Monuments to transportation
Crammed together in one strategic location
Soaring above the salt marsh
My mind wanders through the monotonous traffic
Down to water level
Where I have been in boats
It's easy for me to imagine the swirling brown tide
Coming in under the crossings
Pushing water upriver like a pump
With all the weight of the moon behind it
Unstoppable forces that can't be tamed
I know the turbulent current firsthand
Immensely powerful
Polluted
And deadly
But from up here on the Wittpenn Bridge deck
My view out the windshield is limited
Mostly consisting of concrete
Asphalt
And steel
Except for quick Meadowlands glimpses
Of waving phragmites
Their delicate fluffy seed heads

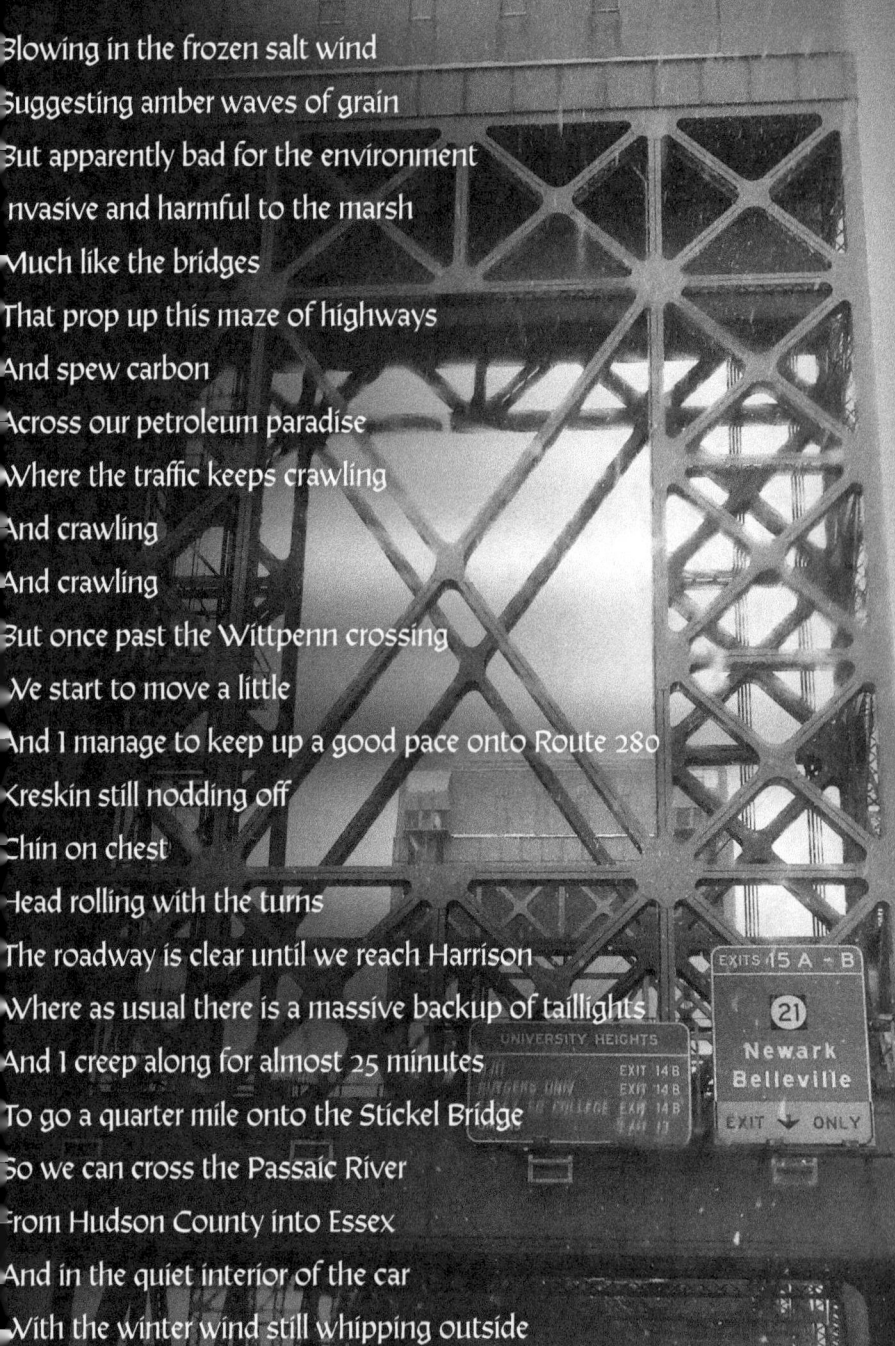

Blowing in the frozen salt wind

Suggesting amber waves of grain

But apparently bad for the environment

Invasive and harmful to the marsh

Much like the bridges

That prop up this maze of highways

And spew carbon

Across our petroleum paradise

Where the traffic keeps crawling

And crawling

And crawling

But once past the Wittpenn crossing

We start to move a little

And I manage to keep up a good pace onto Route 280

Kreskin still nodding off

Chin on chest

Head rolling with the turns

The roadway is clear until we reach Harrison

Where as usual there is a massive backup of taillights

And I creep along for almost 25 minutes

To go a quarter mile onto the Stickel Bridge

So we can cross the Passaic River

From Hudson County into Essex

And in the quiet interior of the car

With the winter wind still whipping outside

I let my mind drift back to summer

When I used to let the boat idle with the current

And float underneath the Stickel
To stare up at the ceaseless traffic
And listen to the thundering of cars and trucks
Their undercarriages briefly exposed through steel mesh
As they sped across the lift portion of the bridge
But winter is too strong for me to sustain my summer revelry
And after waiting in line for what seems like forever
It's finally our turn to drive onto the metal grating
And now it's Kreskin's car that's momentarily on display
Just another one of the many thousands of vehicles
That will flash their chassis
As they cross the bridge tonight
And once we're on the Newark side of the Stickel
The highway mercifully opens up
So I gun the engine into the fast lane
And it isn't long before we're back at Kreskin's house
He wakes up as we turn into the driveway
I grab the mail
Help him get situated inside
And before he can find something else for me to do
I'm back in my own rickety old pickup truck
Speeding home to Montclair
All the while musing in my head
About the sights and sounds of the winter marsh
And the enchanted industrial swamps
Of Northern New Jersey

# # #

EXIT 1

TO 46

Edwards Rd
New Rd

1/2 MILE

FLOOD LAKES

West Essex Park
Along the Passaic
Motor silent and tilted up
Paddling the canoe
Through overflowing woods
Three feet of water in the forest today
Spring snow melt
And severe rain storms
Inundating the swamp
Canopy dripping from recent showers
Soft highway roar
Growing louder
As the *Nightshade* pops from the treeline
Onto the flooded plains of Hatfield Swamp
Usually a field of cattails and grass

Now a sheet of rippling water

So I tilt the motor into the lake

Gas her up

Pull the cord

And cruise

Parallel with Route 280

Where flood water is threatening

To brim over the highway asphalt

But hasn't yet

So the cars keep rolling

While I zoom along

Almost at their level

Crossing the temporary lake

To a bridge over the Whippanong

That allows me to pass under the highway

Onto the flooded fields of Troy Meadows

Vast stretches of grass

Now covered with crystal clear water

Swaying beneath the propeller

As I cut through reflections on the surface

Of overcast skies and bald eagles circling

Ready to defend their nest

In the crook of an ancient tree

That normally stands on the bank

Of the Whippany River

But is now an island in the flood

Two fledgling chicks

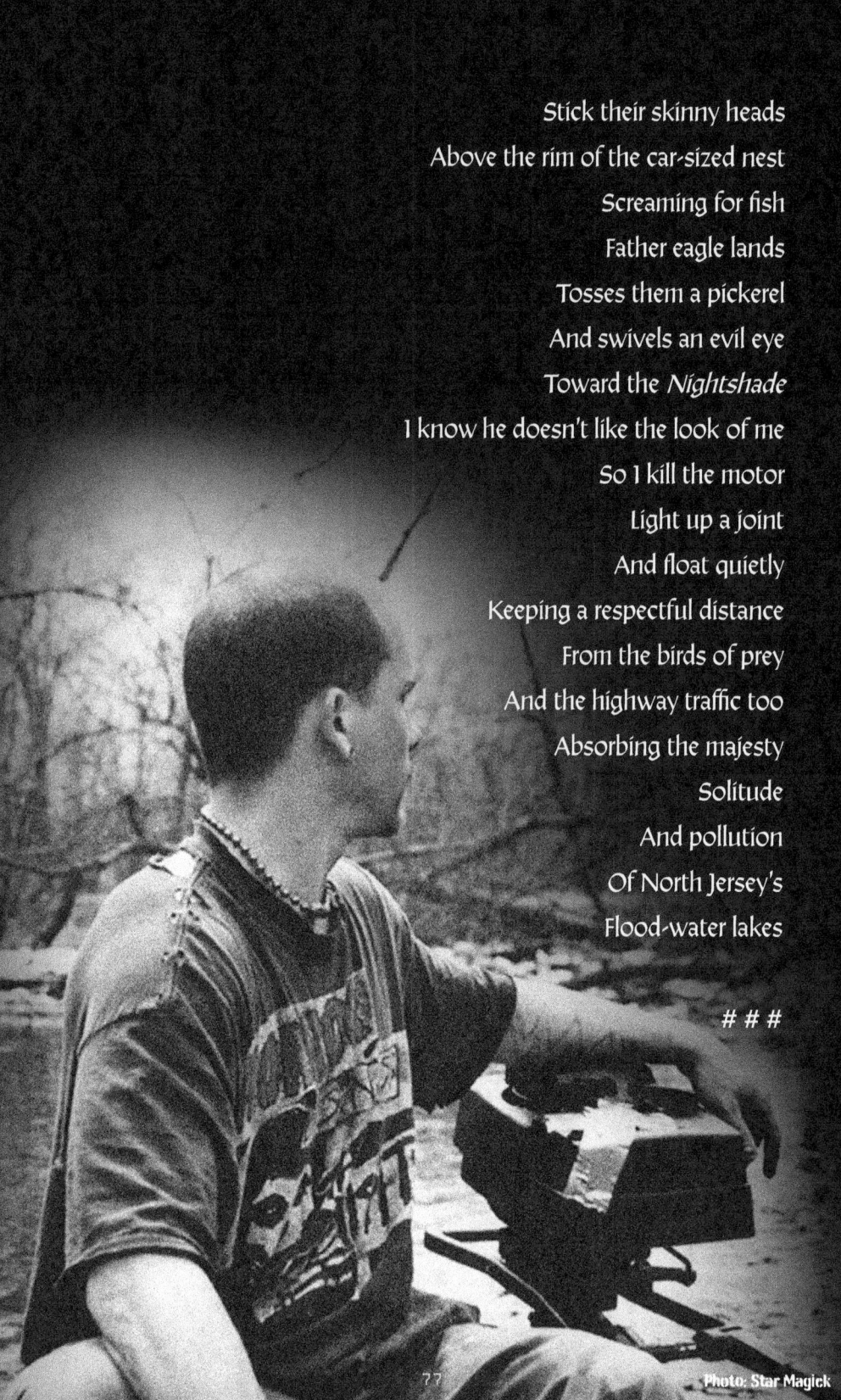

Stick their skinny heads
Above the rim of the car-sized nest
Screaming for fish
Father eagle lands
Tosses them a pickerel
And swivels an evil eye
Toward the *Nightshade*
I know he doesn't like the look of me
So I kill the motor
Light up a joint
And float quietly
Keeping a respectful distance
From the birds of prey
And the highway traffic too
Absorbing the majesty
Solitude
And pollution
Of North Jersey's
Flood-water lakes

# # #

SIGN SPREE

When people see me go by in the boat
They often yell from the shoreline
"Hey, what river is this?"
It's amazing how many people don't know
The name of the stream
Running through their own backyard
So I decided to make a bunch of signs
And hang them along the Passaic
The first step was to make a spray paint stencil
It said:
PASSAIC
RIVER
In bold caps
And had an arrow pointing straight down
To where the river would be

PASSAIC
RIVER↓

I made one hundred 8x10 signs

Out of scavenged plywood

And sprayed the stencil onto each one

Once the signs were mostly dry

I threw a ladder on the rack of my pickup

And set out on a mission

Armed with a cordless drill

A full box of screws

And a hundred Passaic River placards

I was well prepared

For some serious sign-hanging fun

My first target was the Bridge Street Bridge

On the Harrison side of the river

Where I stood on a cement wall in broad daylight

Reaching up on tippy toes

To screw a Passaic River sign to a telephone pole

While people at the traffic light watched

But didn't interfere

That day I covered a lot of territory

Hanging about 60 signs around Newark

Kearny

Lyndhurst

Belleville

Nutley

Clifton

All the arrows on the signs

Pointed directly toward the Passaic

And I felt pretty good about the results
The next day I started in Paterson
Hanging the first sign of the day
Behind Libby's Lunch
And then hopping the fence
At the top of the Great Falls
Where I attached a sign to a tree
75 feet above the river
On the edge of the chasm
This was a sketchy spot
But well worth the risk
Because the Great Falls became a national park
And for some crazy reason
The park rangers let the sign stay
Maybe they didn't want to climb out there and get it
But whatever the rational
It's still hanging to this day
And I like to go there sometimes to visit
But a lot of the other signs
Have been taken down by now
Especially the ones in easy-to-reach places
I can't tell you how many people have emailed me
Saying they stole a Passaic River sign
Only to find out that it was me who put it there
This sign-hanging spree might have gone on indefinitely
But on the third day I got caught
I was out with a fresh batch of 25 additional signs

Making good progress

Filling the gap

Between Paterson and Lyndhurst

Hanging signs in Garfield

Fair Lawn

Elmwood Park

By the time I got to Rutherford

I only had a few signs left

I was busy hanging the last of them

Perched on a ladder in Van Winkle Park

When I heard the *blurp blurp* of a police car

As a cop sped onto the pedestrian path

And aggressively rolled up behind me

My first instinct was to bolt

But my days of running from the police are over

So instead

I climbed down the ladder

Set the drill on the ground

And smiled at the cop

You can only imagine the young officer's confusion

As I began to explain

Why I was wearing paint-splattered coveralls

And hanging Passaic River signs

"Just for fun" on a work day

He kept trying to figure out my angle

Investigating how I might be profiting from this activity

I explained that I'm a frequent boater

That I love the Passaic River
And that I'm seeking to enhance public awareness
He sort of got it, but wasn't sure what to do next
So he radioed headquarters
Asking if he should arrest me
He was given instructions to wait
And soon his commander rolled up
A much older cop with a salt-and-pepper mustache
Who calmly assessed my motives
As I justified the validity of my sign-hanging spree
And backed up my story
With a copy of the *Weird NJ* special issue
Nightshade on the Passaic
He eventually saw I was telling the truth
But made me take the sign down
And then sent me on my way with a warning
Not to hang anymore signs in Rutherford
Which I agreed to
And so far haven't violated
Out of all the signs I hung in the wild
That one was up for the shortest time
Perhaps the best placed signs
Were the ones my buddy Frank and I put up later
From his speedboat *The Jersey Tomato*
We waited for a very high moon tide
And launched at the Snake Hill boat ramp
On the Hackensack River

After cruising through Newark Bay
We came up the mouth of the Passaic
And hung signs for 15 miles
From Kearny Point to Wallington
Motoring slowly up to bulkheads
Bridges
And creosote poles
Where I would stand on the bow of the boat
And attach the signs as high as possible
So when the tide receded
They would be well above the average water level
These covert missions are about as close as I get
To having good clean fun
And I think I feel another sign spree coming on
So if you're walking along the river
Or driving in your car
Make sure to keep your eyes peeled
You might catch a glimpse of Wheeler
As I balance on a ladder
With a screw gun in one hand
And a handmade sign in the other
Trying not to break my neck
While crudely attempting to spread the word
About our most important local resource:
The Passaic River

# # #

HALLOWEEN ON THE PASSAIC

Wood smoke
Salt air
Autumn leaves
Navigating upstream
In the *Sevas Natas*
Keeping the boat at half speed
Through the unmarked channel
Of the Second River Shoal
Between low tide rocks
That could rip out the hull
If not traversed with precision
Laughter floats on the breeze
From early trick or treaters
Making their rounds through Kearny
Beneath an afternoon moon
Shining full circle in the blue sky
Where tonight witches will soar

On broomsticks
To celebrate Samhain
And All Hallows' Eve
But now I'm the one flying
Past the mouth of the shoal
Full speed ahead
Up the Belleville Reach
Leaving a trail of echoes
Under the Rutgers Street Bridge
And a big wake
That soon catches up with me
When I slow down to investigate
An orange blob
Afloat in the drift
Somebody's perfectly good pumpkin
Going out with the tide
I stop and scoop it up
Whip out my knife
And carve a quick jack o'lantern
Right then and there
For the docks
To serve as a beacon
For river spirits
Night haunts
And creatures of the deep

# # #

THE PASSAIC RIVER WILL
TRIUMPH

EXIT 5
Mill St
Belleville
N Newark
NEXT RIGHT

We may think of the Passaic River

As a poisoned

Sewage smeared

Death zone

A place to throw corpses

Dump garbage

And dispose of toxic chemicals

We may think of her as our personal toilet

A sluiceway for all those icky bad things

Expelled from our disgusting bodies

A place where we can flush our daily shame

And never think twice

But there will come a time

When we will be confronted by the fact

That everything on Earth is connected

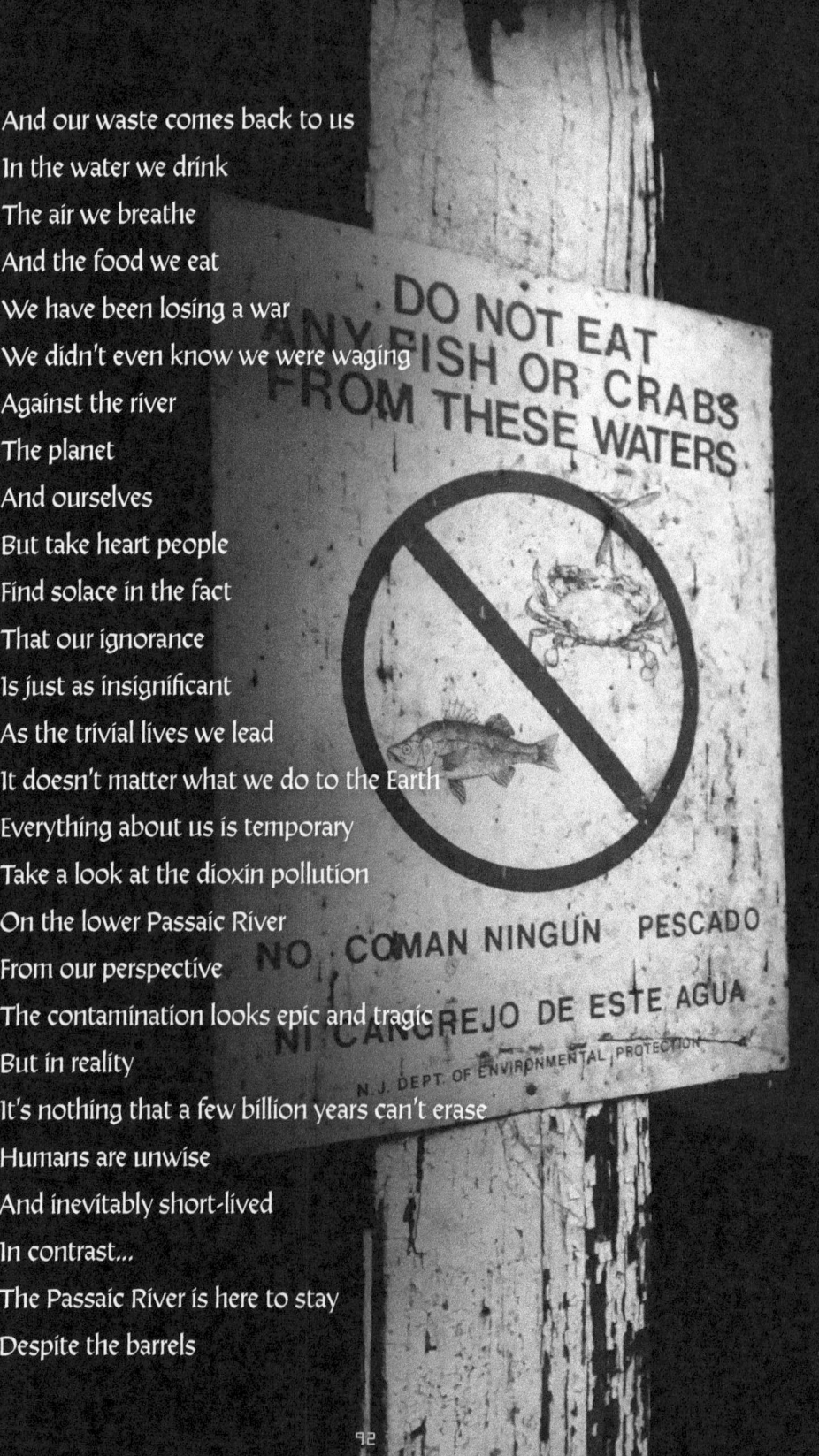

And our waste comes back to us

In the water we drink

The air we breathe

And the food we eat

We have been losing a war

We didn't even know we were waging

Against the river

The planet

And ourselves

But take heart people

Find solace in the fact

That our ignorance

Is just as insignificant

As the trivial lives we lead

It doesn't matter what we do to the Earth

Everything about us is temporary

Take a look at the dioxin pollution

On the lower Passaic River

From our perspective

The contamination looks epic and tragic

But in reality

It's nothing that a few billion years can't erase

Humans are unwise

And inevitably short-lived

In contrast...

The Passaic River is here to stay

Despite the barrels

DO NOT EAT
ANY FISH OR CRABS
FROM THESE WATERS

NO COMAN NINGÚN PESCADO
NI CANGREJO DE ESTE AGUA

N.J. DEPT. OF ENVIRONMENTAL PROTECTION

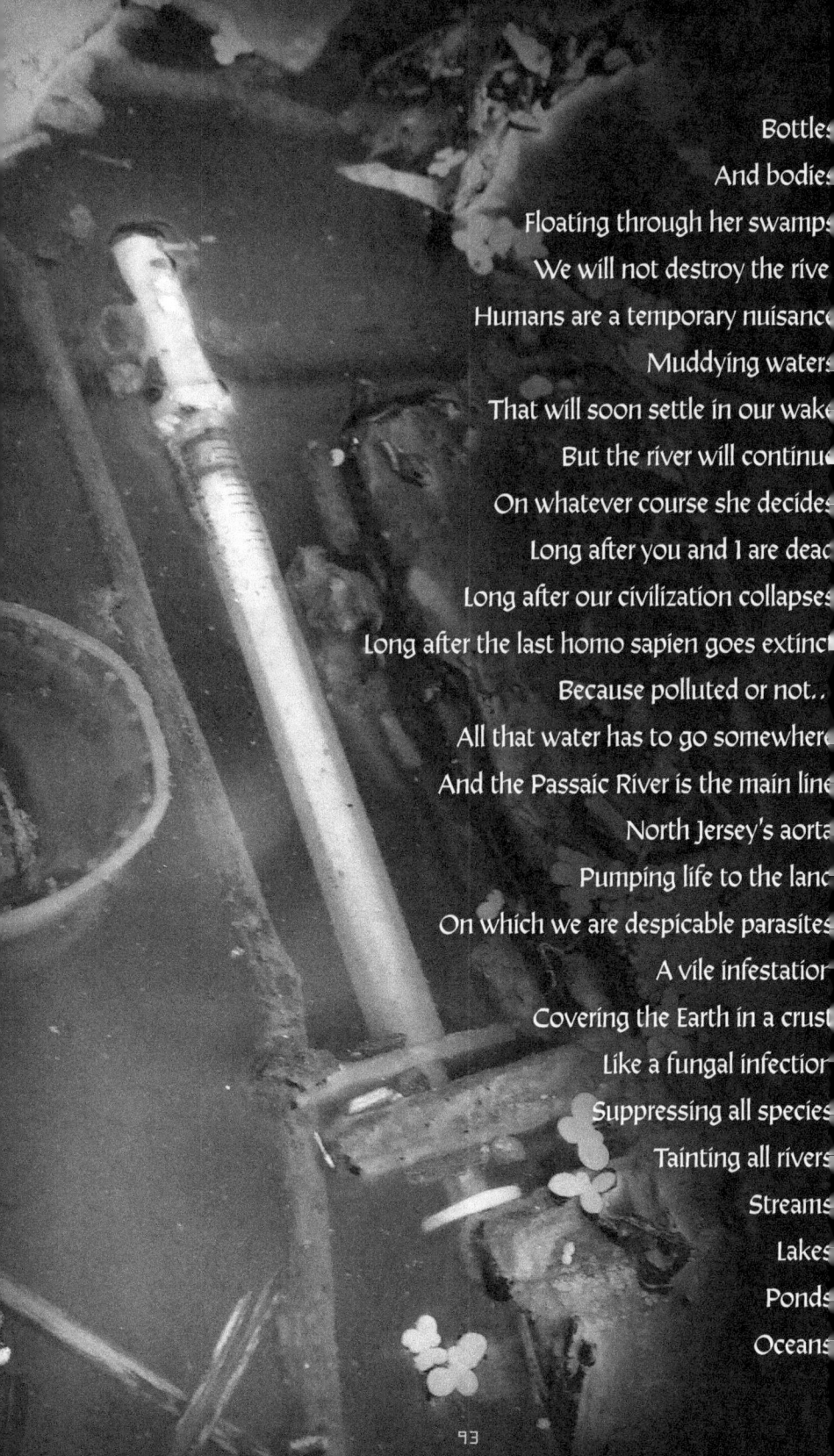

Bottles
And bodies
Floating through her swamps
We will not destroy the river
Humans are a temporary nuisance
Muddying waters
That will soon settle in our wake
But the river will continue
On whatever course she decides
Long after you and I are dead
Long after our civilization collapses
Long after the last homo sapien goes extinct
Because polluted or not..
All that water has to go somewhere
And the Passaic River is the main line
North Jersey's aorta
Pumping life to the land
On which we are despicable parasites
A vile infestation
Covering the Earth in a crust
Like a fungal infection
Suppressing all species
Tainting all rivers
Streams
Lakes
Ponds
Oceans

Seas

Skies

And what will happen

When our warmongering

Against the Earth

Goes too far?

What are all those nuclear missiles for?

Waiting in silos and subs

Ready to perform their duty

Of mutually assured destruction

When the ICBMs start flying

And the cities burn

And the sun goes dark

And the crops won't grow

And the water is vile

And we expire

Along with our families

Irradiated

Starved

Parched

Poisoned

Dead

Maybe we will finally see

That everything is connected

But it will be too late

And here's the really bad news...

It's already too late

Go down to the river right now
You will find signs
Of end times
Our pollution floating on the surface
Can be read like tea leaves
And foretells of doom
Stare long enough into the depths
And you will see visions
Of a panicked human herd
Running off the cliff face of technology
Into a nuclear inferno
Of our own exquisite design
And we'll take every living creature on this planet
Straight to hell with us
But the Passaic River will triumph
She will persist
When we dammed the river
We damned ourselves
But the Passaic will go
And long live her flow

# # #

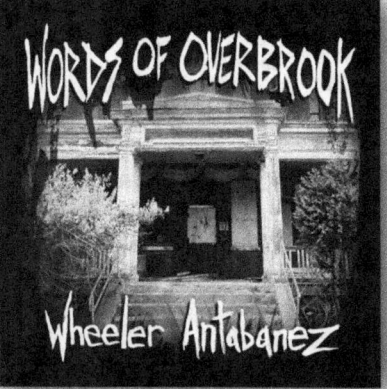

WHEELER ANTABANEZ

Photo: Mike Holland

www.ingramcontent.com/pod-product-compliance
Lightning Source LLC
Chambersburg PA
CBHW070105300526
45788CB00016B/2368